SPORTS AND ATHLETICS PREPARATION, PERFORMANCE AND PSYCHOLOGY

PROFESSIONAL AND COLLEGIATE SPORTS: LEGAL AND TAX ISSUES

SPORTS AND ATHLETICS PREPARATION, PERFORMANCE AND PSYCHOLOGY

Additional books in this series can be found on Nova's website under the Series tab.

Additional E-books in this series can be found on Nova's website under the E-book tab.

SPORTS AND ATHLETICS PREPARATION, PERFORMANCE AND PSYCHOLOGY

PROFESSIONAL AND COLLEGIATE SPORTS: LEGAL AND TAX ISSUES

THOMAS M. MILLER
EDITOR

Nova Science Publishers, Inc.
New York

For permission to use material from this book please contact us:
Telephone 631-231-7269; Fax 631-231-8175
Web Site: http://www.novapublishers.com

LIBRARY OF CONGRESS CATALOGING-IN-PUBLICATION DATA

Professional and collegiate sports : legal and tax issues / editor, Thomas M. Miller.
p. cm.
Includes bibliographical references and index.
ISBN 978-1-61122-191-6 (softcover)
1. Professional sports--Law and legislation--United States. 2. College sports--Law and legislation--United States. 3. Sports--Taxation--Law and legislation--United States. I. Miller, Thomas M.
KF3989.P76 2010
344.73'099--dc22

2010038654

Published by Nova Science Publishers, Inc. ✢ New York

CONTENTS

PREFACE

This book provides an examination of professional and legal sports today with a focus on the congressional response to selected work stoppages in professional sports; the manufacturing, licensing and marketing of team and league-logoed and trademarked clothing and merchandise; and the issue of tax preferences for collegiate sports.

Chapter 1- The National Football League's (NFL) collective bargaining agreement (CBA) was set to expire in 2012. In May 2008, the owners voted unanimously to terminate the agreement early, an option that was available to either party to the CBA. If the NFL and the NFL Players Association (NFLPA) do not have a new CBA in place prior to the 2010-2011 season, there will be no salary cap for that season. The union has indicated that it expects the owners to impose a lockout in 2011.

Given the status of labor-management relations in professional football, a number of questions have been raised. Of particular interest to some observers is how Congress responded in the past to work stoppages in professional sports. In attempting to address this particular question, this chapter examines congressional responses to the two most recent work stoppages in the NFL, which occurred in 1982 and 1987. This chapter also examines the 1994 Major League Baseball strike, which also is useful considering the extent of congressional activity surrounding this strike.

Chapter 2- In a decision that had the potential to upset decades of antitrust law, and also to have a broad impact beyond the immediate consequences for the litigating parties, the Supreme Court ruled, on May 24, 2010, that the intellectual-property licensing activities of the National Football League (NFL or League) and its member teams must be treated as those of separate entities whose cooperation and joint decisions are amenable to antitrust prosecution under Section 1 of the Sherman Act, which prohibits contracts or conspiracies "in restraint of trade" (*American Needle, Inc. v. National Football League,* 560 U.S. ___ (2010)). There had been some concern that a contrary ruling—a finding that the NFL's member teams are but "divisions" of an unincorporated NFL and so are incapable of ever conspiring with either each other or the League itself—could have affected existing antitrust jurisprudence concerning the status of entities in sports leagues generally, and also of those entities involved in cooperative or joint venture activity in such diverse areas as real estate services, financial services, and health care.

Chapter 3- Colleges and universities generally qualify for preferential treatment under the federal income tax. The income of nonprofit private and public postsecondary schools is exempt from taxation, and gifts to those schools are generally tax-deductible to the donor. Those tax preferences stem from the schools' educational mission. But concerns have arisen that some activities undertaken by colleges and universities are only loosely connected to educating students and might be viewed as unrelated to the schools' tax-favored purpose.

In: Professional and Collegiate Sports
Editor: Thomas M. Miller
ISBN: 978-1-61122-191-6

Chapter 1

Congressional Responses to Selected Work Stoppages in Professional Sports

L. Elaine Halchin, Justin Murray, Janice E. Rubin and Jon O. Shimabukuro

Summary

The National Football League's (NFL) collective bargaining agreement (CBA) was set to expire in 2012. In May 2008, the owners voted unanimously to terminate the agreement early, an option that was available to either party to the CBA. If the NFL and the NFL Players Association (NFLPA) do not have a new CBA in place prior to the 2010-2011 season, there will be no salary cap for that season. The union has indicated that it expects the owners to impose a lockout in 2011.

Given the status of labor-management relations in professional football, a number of questions have been raised. Of particular interest to some observers is how Congress responded in the past to work stoppages in professional sports. In attempting to address this particular question, this chapter examines congressional responses to the two most recent work stoppages in the NFL, which occurred in 1982 and 1987. This chapter also examines the 1994 Major

League Baseball strike, which also is useful considering the extent of congressional activity surrounding this strike.

Compared to the 1994 baseball strike, the 1982 and 1987 football strikes did not garner much attention from Congress in terms of legislative measures and hearings. Three legislative measures were introduced in response to the 1982 strike; one was introduced in response to the 1987 strike. Members introduced or offered 22 legislative measures and held five hearings that were related to the baseball strike. With one exception (S.Res. 294, 100th Congress), none of these measures was approved by either house.

Members who introduced, or otherwise supported, legislative measures offered reasons for promoting congressional intervention. Their arguments touched on, for example, the economic impact of work stoppages, the role of baseball's antitrust exemption in establishing a climate conducive to players' strikes, previous congressional involvement in professional sports, and a responsibility to ensure the continuity of football (or baseball).

Disagreeing that congressional intervention was warranted, other Members offered several reasons why Congress ought not to intervene. For example, one Member suggested that repealing baseball's antitrust exemption would alter the balance of power in professional baseball. Other Members believed that more pressing matters deserved Congress's attention. At least one Member suggested that a particular bill, if enacted, would have the effect of favoring the players over the owners.

A summary of NFL labor-management history may be found in **Appendix A. Appendix B** provides an overview of key aspects of labor-management relations and sports, and **Appendix C** includes a discussion of antitrust exemptions applicable to professional sports.

INTRODUCTION

Recent developments in professional football's labor-management relations—specifically, the National Football League (NFL) owners' decision to opt out of the current collective bargaining agreement (CBA)—have prompted questions regarding how, when, and in what manner a new CBA might be drafted. Interest in this matter includes, on the part of some observers, questions about how Congress responded to previous work stoppages in professional sports. In an effort to address this particular question, this chapter examines congressional activity related to the two most recent NFL strikes, which occurred in 1982 and 1987, and the 1994 Major League Baseball (MLB) strike. Although the latter strike involved another professional sports league, it is potentially instructive given the extent of congressional activity surrounding the 1994 strike.

National Football League—Status of Labor-Management Relations

The National Football League's collective bargaining agreement took effect on March 8, 2006, and was to expire on the "last day of the 2012 League Year."[1] As described in the following excerpt from the CBA, however, either party to the agreement could opt to terminate it prior to the established expiration date:

> ***Section 3.* Termination Prior to Expiration Date:**
> (a) Either the NFLPA [NFL Players Association] or the Management Council may terminate both of the final two Capped Years (2010 and 2011) by giving written notice to the other on or before November 8, 2008. In that event, the 2010 League Year would be the Final League Year, and the Agreement would continue in full force and effect until the last day of that League Year, except for the provisions related to the Draft, which would expire as prescribed in Article XVI, Section 1 [of the CBA].[2]

In May 2008, NFL team owners voted unanimously to opt out of the CBA and negotiate a new agreement for the 2011 season and subsequent seasons.[3] If a new agreement is not in place prior to the 2010 season, there will be no salary cap for that season and the current CBA "would expire at the end of the 2010 league year."[4] Reportedly, the NFL Players Association expects NFL owners to impose a lockout in 2011 if a new agreement is not in place by then.[5]

Work Stoppages in Selected Professional Sports Leagues

Work stoppages involving professional sports, whether caused by the players going on strike or the owners imposing a lockout, are by their very nature contentious and not always resolved quickly or easily. Through early 2010, the four major professional sports leagues in the United States—Major

League Baseball (MLB), National Basketball Association (NBA), National Football League, and National Hockey League (NHL)—had experienced a total of 18 work stoppages. **Table 1, Table 2, Table 3**, and **Table 4** list the work stoppages for each sport.

Table 1. M LB Work Stoppages

Year(s)	Type of Work Stoppage	Duration
1972	Strike	13 days
1973	Lockout	17 days
1976	Lockout	17 days
1980	Strike	8 days
1981	Strike	50 days
1985	Strike	2 days
1990	Lockout	32 days
1994-1995	Strike	232 days

Sources: Major League Baseball, "Collective Bargaining, Labor Timeline," at http://mlb.mlb.com/mlb/news/labor/y2006/index.jsp?content=timeline; Associated Press, "Labor Relations; Fehr: Atmosphere Not As 'Poisoned'" As in 1994," *CNNSI.com*, February 25, 2001, at http://sportsillustrated.cnn.com/ baseball/ mlb/news/2001/02/25/ fehr_labor_ap/; "Labor Matters: Unions," *The Business of Sports*, ed. Scott R. Rosner and Kenneth L. Shropshire (Boston: Jones and Bartlett, 2004), p. 200.

Notes: The Major League Baseball Players Association (MLBPA) became a labor union in 1966. (Major League Baseball Players Association, "MLBPA Info: Frequently Asked Questions," at http://mlbplayers.mlb.com/pa/info/ faq.jsp#created.) The current CBA expires on December 11, 2011. (Major League Baseball Players Association, "MLBPA Info: Basic Agreement," at http://mlbplayers.mlb.com/pa/info/cba.jsp.)

Table 2. NBA Work Stoppages

Year(s)	Type of Work Stoppage	Duration
1995	Lockout	77 days
1998-1999	Lockout	191 days

Source: "Labor Matters: Unions," *The Business of Sports*, ed. Scott R. Rosner and Kenneth L. Shropshire (Boston: Jones and Bartlett2004), p. 200.

Notes: The National Basketball Players Association (NBPA) was established in 1954. (National Basketball Players' Association, "NBPA History," at http://www.nbpa.com/ history.php.) The current CBA "runs through the 2010-11 season." (David Aldridge, "Several Issues Will Come to Head During the NBA Labor Talks," August 4, 2009, at http://www.nba.com/2009/news/ features/david_ aldridge/08/04/ aldridge.labor/ index. html.)

Table 3. NFL Work Stoppages

Year(s)	Type of Work Stoppage	Duration
1968	Lockout followed by a strike	10 days
1970	Lockout followed by a strike	20 days
1974	Strike	42 days
1982	Strike	57 days
1987	Strike	24 days

Sources: Paul D. Staudohar, *Playing for Dollars: Labor Relations and the Sports Business*, 3rd ed. (Ithaca, NY: Cornell University Press, 1996), pp. 71-72; Associated Press, "N.F.L. Players Back on Jobs," *New York Times*, October 20,1987, at https://w3.nexis.com, p. B8; William C. Rhoden, "Jets Roar Past Patriots as Season Comes to a Pause," *New York Times*, September 22, 1987, at https://w3.nexis.com, p. A29; NFL Players Association, "History, The 1970's – AFL and NFL Players Associations Merge," at http://www.nflplayers.com/user/ template.aspx?fmid=1 82&lmid=239&pid=1 036&type=c; NFL Players Association, "History, The 1960's – ALF/NFL Competition," at http://www. nflplayers. com/user/template.aspx? fmid=182 &lmid= 239&pid=1033&type=c; "Labor Matters: Unions," *The Business of Sports*, ed. Scott R. Rosner and Kenneth L. Shropshire (Boston: Jones and Bartlett2004), p. 200.

Notes: The NFL Players Association (NFLPA) was established in 1956. (NFL Players Association, "History, The Beginning – 1956," at http://nflplayers.com/user/ template.aspx?fmid=182&lmid=239&pid=1915&type=c.) However, it was not until 1970 that the AFL Players Association and the NFL Players Association merged, retaining the name of the latter and becoming a recognized union. (NFL Players Association, "History, The 1970's – AFL and NFL Players Associations Merge," at http://nflplayers.com/ user/template.aspx?fmid=182&lmid= 239 & pid= 1 036&type=c.)

Table 4. NHL Work Stoppages

Year(s)	Type of Work Stoppage	Duration
1992	Strike	10 days
1994-1995	Lockout	103 days
2004-2005	Lockout	302 days

Sources: Paul D. Staudohar, *Playing for Dollars: Labor Relations and the Sports Business*, 3rd ed. (Ithaca, NY: Cornell University Press, 1996), p. 151; Associated Press,"NHL Lockout Chronology," February 16, 2005, at http://sports.espn.go.com/nhl/news/story?id=1993004; Joe LaPointe, "Play Hockey! Settlement Ends 10-Day Strike," *New York Times*, April 11, 1992, at http://www.nytimes.com/1992/04/11/sports/hockey-play-hockeysettlement-ends-10-day-strike.html?scp=46&sq=Bob+Goodenow&st=nyt; Associated Press, "NHL Lockout Chronology," *USA Today.com*, July 13, 2005, at http://www.usatoday.com/ sports/hockey/nhl/2005-07-13-lockout-chronology_x.htm; "Labor Matters: Unions,"

The Business of Sports, ed. Scott R. Rosner and Kenneth L. Shropshire (Boston: Jones and Bartlett2004), p. 200.

Notes: The National Hockey League Players' Association was established in 1967. (National Hockey League Players' Association, "What Is the NHLPA?" at http://www.nhlpa.com/AboutTheNHLPA/WhatIs.asp.) The current CBA expires in 2011. (National Hockey League, "NHL Players Association Will Not Reopen CBA," January 23, 2009, at http://www.nhl.com/ice

Major League Baseball has experienced the greatest number of work stoppages (eight), followed by the NFL (five), NHL (three), and NBA (two). While both NBA work stoppages were lockouts, the other three leagues have experienced a combination of strikes and lockouts. Major League Baseball has had five strikes and three lockouts, and the NHL one strike and two lockouts. The NFL is somewhat unusual in that two of its five work stoppages began as lockouts and concluded as strikes (1968 and 1970). The average length of work stoppages for each league is as follows: MLB, 46 days (excluding the 232-day strike, the average is 20 days); NBA, 134 days; NFL, 31 days; and NHL, 138 days (excluding the 10-day strike, the average is 203 days).[6] The medians for the four leagues are as follows: MLB, 17 days; NBA, 134 days; NFL, 24 days; and NHL, 103 days.

In the following three sections, this chapter describes congressional responses to the 1982 and 1987 NFL strikes and the 1994 MLB strike, respectively. The latter section also includes a discussion of the Clinton Administration's attempts to facilitate the resolution of the baseball strike. A summary of the circumstances of each strike is followed by a table that identifies relevant legislative measures, and an overview of Members' comments and report language regarding the strike, which were drawn from congressional hearings and reports, and remarks made on the House or Senate floor. This information shows the extent of actual, or intended, congressional involvement and how some Members viewed congressional involvement in the strike. A summary of NFL labor-management history may be found in **Appendix A. Appendix B** provides an overview of key aspects of labor-management relations and sports, and **Appendix C** includes a discussion of antitrust exemptions applicable to professional sports.

Table 5. 97th Congress: Legislative Measures Related to the 1982 NFL Strike

Legislative Measure (Congress)	Brief Summary	Hearing Held or Written Report Published?	Number of Cosponsors	Final Major Action
H.Res. 597 (97th)	Support a prompt settlement of the NFL strike.	No	0	House Committee on Education and Labor referred the bill to the Subcommittee on Labor- Management Relations.
H.Res. 598 (97th)	Support a prompt settlement of the NFL strike.	No	14	House Committee on Education and Labor referred the bill to the Subcommittee on Labor- Management Relations.
S. 3003 (97th)	Establish a final offer arbitration procedure for labor disputes involving professional baseball, basketball, football, and hockey.[a]	No	0	Senate Committee on Labor and Human Resources referred the bill to the Subcommittee on Labor and requested comment from the Department of Labor and the Office of Management and Budget.

Source: Legislative Information System, at http://www.congress.gov.

Note:

a. This bill also would have required the parties to the current NFL strike "to resume activities" and authorized the President to direct them to submit final offers in accordance with Sec. 2 of S. 3003 within five days of the date of enactment.

1982 National Football League Strike

On September 20, 1982, NFL players voted to strike after negotiations for a new collective bargaining agreement broke down. The previous CBA had expired on July 15, 1982. Initially, the NFL Players Association (NFLPA) sought 55% of the owners' gross revenues. The NFL rejected the players association's demands and offered to share $1.6 billion with the NFLPA over five years. The dispute was resolved when the players association accepted the owners' offer to share $1.28 billion over five years and to provide $60 million to the union to compensate players for salaries not paid during the strike. The season resumed on November 21, 1982. On December 5, 1982, the players association and the owners signed a new five-year CBA. After the strike was resolved, the season resumed with a seven-game regular season schedule and an expanded playoff bracket, which culminated in Super Bowl XVI on January 30, 1983. [7]

Congressional Response

Table 5 shows the legislative measures that were introduced in response to the strike.

H.Res. 597 and H.Res. 598[8] (97th Congress)

Either resolution, if passed, would have urged the parties to take steps to promptly settle the strike and resume the season.

S. 3003, Organized Professional Team Sports Labor Dispute Resolution Act of 1982 (97th Congress)

Although no hearings were held, the bill's sponsor, Senator Ted Stevens, offered a rationale for congressional involvement when he introduced S. 3003. Noting that "Congress has clearly established a history of promoting the public interest in professional sports," he then mentioned several instances when legislation involving professional sports was enacted.[9]

> For example, in 1973, we adopted legislation calling for the telecasting of sold-out home games of professional sports teams. We also enacted legislation encouraging the stability of professional sports leagues by confirming, in 1961, the right of professional sport leagues to jointly sell their television rights to the national networks. In 1966, we authorized the

> consolidation of the American Football League and the National Football League so that football franchises could continue to operate on a stable basis in their resident communities. Thus we have long recognized the public interest in encouraging professional sports, and have affirmatively acted to encourage the financial stability of the leagues.[10]

Senator Stevens also noted the adverse economic consequences of the football strike, mentioning that the "strike produced major economic disruptions and losses in all of the communities which host NFL teams."[11]

1987 National Football League Strike

The 1982 CBA expired on August 31, 1987, and shortly thereafter negotiations broke down between the NFLPA and the NFL over the issue of free agency and other matters. The union voted to strike on September 22, 1987. The owners cancelled the games scheduled for September 26 and September 27, 1987, while announcing their intention to resume the season on October 4, 1987, with replacement players. NFL players who did not share the union's concerns regarding free agency, or who needed the money, played alongside the replacement players.[12]

The striking players voted to return to work on October 15, 1987, even though there was no CBA. Team owners, however, banned players who had not agreed to return to work by the ownerimposed deadline of October 14, 1987, from participating in that week's scheduled games. Thus, striking players who did not return to their teams until after the NFLPA vote lost an additional week of pay. Replacement players were released as the regular players returned to their jobs. The 1987-1988 season concluded on January 31, 1988, when the Super Bowl was held at Jack Murphy Stadium in San Diego.

Congressional Response

Table 6 shows the legislative measure that was introduced in response to the strike.

Table 6. 100th Congress: Legislative Measure Related to the 1987 NFL Strike

Legislative Measure (Congress)	Brief Summary	Hearing Held or Written Report Published?	Number of Cosponsors	Final Major Action
S.Res. 294 (100th)	Support a prompt settlement of the NFL strike.	No	2	Agreed to by voice vote.

Source: Legislative Information System, at http://www.congress.gov.

S.Res. 294, which was agreed to without amendment by a voice vote, called on both parties—the players association and the NFL Management Council—to resume negotiations.[13]

Although S.Res. 291 (100th Congress), which addressed the telecasting practices of the NFL, was not a response to the NFL players' strike, the subject was broached during a hearing on the resolution.[14] Following his introduction of Pete Rozelle, then-commissioner of the NFL, the subcommittee's chairman initiated the following exchange with Rozelle regarding the ongoing strike:

> Senator METZENBAUM. Mr. Rozelle, as I indicated to you before the hearing, I think for us to have you before this hearing and not inquire of you as to why you as the Commissioner have not been heard from in connection with some effort to settle the strike between the players and the NFL, would be surprising to the many people in this country that are asking that question. I wonder if you would be good enough to tell us why you as the Commissioner have not seen fit to move in and at least attempt to mediate the issue.
>
> Mr. ROZELLE. I have had meetings with the President of the Players' Association, Gene Upshaw, and phone conversations. I have attempted to stay close to the situation, of course, on the owners' Management Council side. There has been a very, very strong disagreement on several issues that have inhibited the negotiating process. I am pleased now that I think that perhaps certain pressures are involved on both sides, and I understand they are going to be meeting promptly to get back into negotiating. I think it is unfortunate they could not have accomplished more back in May, June and July, but it was all the thrust at once when the season came on us.
>
> Senate METZENBAUM. Well, I might say I think that all of us are pleased to know that management and players are going back to the negotiating table. I never heard of a strike that was settled without direct negotiations, oftentimes through some mediator—whether it is from the U.S. Mediation and Conciliation Service or someone else.... The American people

have a strong interest in this issue. They do not have an ownership right, but they feel they have some type of right in professional football. And I think the sooner the matter gets resolved and the parties themselves meet together and resolve it, I think the happier the American people will be. I think it will be one less issue to be on the top of the news in the nightly news every night.[15]

In an exchange that occurred later in the hearing, Senator Arlen Specter similarly encouraged the NFL commissioner to assist in settling the strike. The relevant excerpt is as follows:

Senator SPECTER. Okay. I would like to disagree with Senator Hatch, even though he is gone, on one small point. That is about the adequacy of the substitute games on this past Sunday. I would join my colleague, Senator Metzenbaum, Commissioner Rozelle, in urging you to do everything you could personally to lend your good offices to settle the strike. You have been a very powerful force in the National Football League for many, many years. I believe you became Commissioner in the 1950s.

Mr. ROZELLE. 1960, Senator.

Senator SPECTER. 1960. Okay. But you have been the Commissioner for 27 years, one of the toughest jobs around, pulled together the National Football League in an era of extraordinary growth and extraordinary complexity, and you have appeared before this Judiciary Committee on many occasions in my short tenure in the United States Senate. I think you have always done a very able job, and I think you have done a very able job here this morning. I would very much like to see your talents used this afternoon to settle the football strike.

Mr. ROZELLE. I would love to, believe me. It is so terribly frustrating, Senator.

Mr. MODELL. I would like to add a thought in that regard. Yes, I echo your sentiments on what he has done for 26, 27 years. But if the players were to accept him as a neutral Commissioner, which he really is, this strike never would have gotten off the ground. They view him as an owners' appointee, and that gives us great difficulty.[16]

Senator SPECTER. Well, the strike has gotten off the ground, but I think it is a little different ball game today than it was a week ago. We have had a week of substitute players. I think the American public is totally dissatisfied with that. There have been incidents around the league which are not a credit for anybody. And I think it is time it came to a close. If there is one man who could probably do it better than anyone else, if anybody could do it, it is Commissioner Rozelle. So we are going to let you go early, Commissioner.[17]

1994 Major League Baseball Strike

Unable to reach an agreement with the owners on a new CBA in summer 1994, major league players voted, on August 12, 1994, to strike. Approximately one month later, on September 14, 1994, Major League Baseball cancelled the remainder of the season. The decisions to strike and to cancel the season followed several months of negotiations over a number of issues, including baseball's revenue sharing plan. Beginning in fall 1994, the Clinton Administration attempted to facilitate negotiations between the parties.[18] The work stoppage ended in early 1995 following then-U.S. District Court Judge Sonia Sotomayor's issuance of an injunction that had been "requested by the National Labor Relations Board ordering baseball owners to restore bidding on free agents, a resumption and salary arbitration and the anti-collusion rules which were a part" of the CBA that had expired the previous year.[19] Shortly after Judge Sotomayor issued the injunction, which occurred on March 31, 1995, major league baseball owners "accepted the players' offer to return to work."[20] Although the commencement of the 1995 season was delayed, beginning on April 26 instead of April 3, which was the original opening day, the season was played without interruption and the postseason concluded with the World Series.[21]

Congressional Response

Table 7 shows the legislative measures that were introduced in response to the strike.

S. 2380, H.R. 4965, and S.Amdt. 2601 to H.R. 4649, Baseball Fans Protection Act of 1994 (103rd Congress)

Senator Howard Metzenbaum introduced S. 2380 and offered S.Amdt. 2601. H.R. 4649 was a companion bill to S. 2380.

Senator Metzenbaum believed that "revoking the owners' antitrust immunity is the best long-term solution to the mess the players and the owners have made of major league baseball," but he decided to offer instead what he characterized as a "compromise bill."[22] He went on to explain his reasoning as follows:

Table 7. 103rd and 104th Congresses: Legislative Measures and Hearing Related to the 1994 MLB Strike

Legislative Measure or Hearing (Congress)	Brief Summary	Hearing Held or Written Report Published?	Number of Cosponsors	Final Major Action
S. 2380 (103rd)[a]	Apply antitrust laws to a term or condition unilaterally imposed by any party to the MLB CBA.	No	3	Placed on the Senate Legislative Calendar under General Orders.
S.Amdt. 2601 to H.R. 4649 (103rd)	Apply antitrust laws to a term or condition unilaterally imposed by any party to the MLB CBA.	No	1	Withdrawn in the Senate.
H.R. 4965 (103rd)[a]	Apply antitrust laws to a term or condition unilaterally imposed by any party to the MLB CBA.	No	0	House Committee on the Judiciary referred the bill to the Subcommittee on Economic and Commercial Law.
S. 2401 (103rd)	Establish a National Commission on Major League Baseball to oversee and regulate MLB, including the conduct of binding arbitration in the event of a labor impasse.	No	0	Referred to the Senate Committee on Commerce.
H.R. 4994 (103rd)	Apply antitrust laws to term(s) or condition(s) unilaterally imposed by any party to the MLB CBA.	Yes	6	Placed on the Union Calendar.
H.R. 5095 (103rd)	Effective February 1, 1995, establish an arbitration board to conduct binding arbitration for MLB owners and players.	Yes	0	House Committee on Education and Labor requested executive comment from Labor.[b]

Table 7. (Continued)

Legislative Measure or Hearing (Congress)	Brief Summary	Hearing Held or Written Report Published?	Number of Cosponsors	Final Major Action
House Committee on the Judiciary, Subcommittee on Economic and Commercial Law (103rd)	Major League Baseball's antitrust exemption and its relationship to the ongoing strike.	Yes	Not applicable	Hearing published in 1994.
H.R. 45 (104th)	Apply antitrust laws to a term or condition unilaterally imposed by any party to the MLB CBA.	No	0	Referred to the House Committee on the Judiciary.
H.R. 105 (104th)	Exclude professional baseball from the antitrust exemption applicable to certain television contracts.	No	0	Referred to the House Committee on the Judiciary.
H.R. 106 (104th)	Apply antitrust laws to professional baseball teams and leagues.	No	7	Referred to the House Committee on the Judiciary.
H.R. 120 (104th)	Apply antitrust laws to term(s) or condition(s) unilaterally imposed by any party to the MLB CBA.	No	9	Referred to the House Committee on the Judiciary.

Table 7. (Continued)

Legislative Measure or Hearing (Congress)	Brief Summary	Hearing Held or Written Report Published?	Number of Cosponsors	Final Major Action
H.R. 365 (104th)	Apply antitrust laws to term(s) or condition(s) unilaterally imposed by any party to the MLB CBA.	No	0	Referred to the House Committee on the Judiciary.
H.R. 386 (104th)	Apply antitrust laws to professional baseball.	No	3	Referred to the House Committee on the Judiciary.
H.R. 397 (104th)	Effective February 1, 1995, establish an arbitration board to conduct binding arbitration for MLB owners and players.	No	0	House Committee on Economic and Educational Opportunities referred the bill to the Subcommittee on Employer- Employee Relations.
H.R. 735 (104th)	Establish a National Commission on Professional Baseball to oversee and investigate major league and minor league baseball, including the conduct of binding arbitration in the event of a labor impasse between MLB and players.	No	0	Referred to the House Committee on the Judiciary. Referred by the House Committee on Commerce to the Subcommittee on Commerce, Trade, and Hazardous Materials. Referred by the House Committee on Economic and Educational Opportunities to the Subcommittee on Employer-Employee Relations.
H.R. 749 (104th)	Apply antitrust laws to professional baseball teams and leagues.	No	0	Referred to the House Committee on the Judiciary.

Table 7. (Continued)

Legislative Measure or Hearing (Congress)	Brief Summary	Hearing Held or Written Report Published?	Number of Cosponsors	Final Major Action
H.R. 870 (104th)[c]	Establish a National Baseball Dispute Resolution Panel, which shall resolve the current labor dispute by setting forth a binding agreement.	No	6	House Committee on Economic and Educational Opportunities referred the bill to the Subcommittee on Employer- Employee Relations.
H.R. 1612 (104th)	Apply antitrust laws to professional baseball.	No	6	Referred to the House Committee on the Judiciary.
S. 15 (104th)	Except as provided in P.L. 87-331 (Sports Broadcasting Act of 1961), apply antitrust laws to professional baseball.	No	2	Referred to the Senate Committee on the Judiciary.
S. 376 (104th)[c]	Establish a National Baseball Dispute Resolution Panel, which shall resolve the current labor dispute by setting forth a binding agreement.	No	1	Placed on Senate Legislative Calendar under General Orders.
S. 415 (104th)	Apply antitrust laws to profess-ional baseball's labor relations.	Yes[d]	4	Hearing held by the Senate Commi-ttee on the Judiciary, Subcommittee on Antitrust and Business.
S. 416 (104th)	Apply antitrust laws to professional major league baseball.	Yes[d]	1	Hearing held by the Senate Committee on the Judiciary, Subcommittee on Antitrust and Business.

Table 7. (Continued)

Legislative Measure or Hearing (Congress)	Brief Summary	Hearing Held or Written Report Published?	Number of Cosponsors	Final Major Action
S. 627 (104th)	Apply antitrust laws to professional major league baseball.	Yes	4	Placed on Senate Legislative Calendar under General Orders.

Source: Legislative Information System, at http://www.congress.gov. Notes:

a. S. 2380 and H.R. 4965 were companion bills.

b. This appears to be a reference to the Department of Labor.

c. H.R. 870 and S. 376 were companion bills.

d. One hearing was held for S. 415 and S. 416.

> It [S. 2380] does not eliminate the players right to strike, or the owners right to lock them out. Instead, the bill allows the antitrust laws to be invoked if the owners impose a salary cap or any other terms and conditions on the players. This should take away the owners' incentive to play hard ball and impose unilateral conditions. It should also relieve players' fear that they need to strike in order to prevent a salary cap from being shoved down their throats when the season ends. Once the owners and players resolve their differences and sign a new agreement, the bill expires....[23]
>
> Right now, the big league players cannot use the antitrust laws. If they could, the owners would have to deal with them fairly or face the consequences in a court of law. In other words, what this bill does is give the players another tool they can use to avoid striking, or to bring a strike to a quick end. The last seven times the baseball players and owners have met at the bargaining table there has been a work stoppage: A strike or lockout. This has not happened in other professional sports because those players could use the antitrust laws to settle labor disputes.... If the antitrust laws applied to baseball, the owners could not force the players to accept unreasonable terms and conditions if their labor negotiations hit impasse. The players could challenge the owners unreasonable demands by launching an antitrust suit instead of shutting down the season.[24]

Senator Orrin Hatch, who co-sponsored S. 2380, encouraged both sides to resolve their differences, and, unlike Senator Metzenbaum, did not support the blanket repeal of major league baseball's antitrust immunity.[25] Couching the barriers to resolution as the result of a "legal anomaly," Senator Hatch offered the following explanation of his position:

> On the one hand, professional baseball enjoys a unique and longstanding immunity from the antitrust laws. I have opposed repeal of this immunity, and I continue to do so. On the other hand, the owners retain the right under our current labor laws to impose unilaterally new terms and conditions of employment once an impasse in the bargaining has been reached. I am concerned that the unique combination of these two legal roles, which occurs in no other industry, has the effect of inviting delay and of discouraging prompt resolution of the pending labor dispute. The Baseball Fans Protection Act that Senator Metzenbaum and I are introducing would correct this legal anomaly.[26]

The sponsor of H.R. 4965, Representative Major R. Owens, did not provide any remarks when he introduced his bill.

S. 2401, National Commission on Major League Baseball Act of 1994 (103rd Congress)

Introduced by Senator Dennis DeConcini, S. 2401, if enacted, would have established a commission on professional baseball. Major League Baseball did not have a commissioner at the time of the strike, and Senator DeConcini envisioned the panel serving as an "impartial commissioner" that would "give the fans a much needed voice in the debate."[27] Among the many responsibilities he set forth for the proposed commission, he noted that "[m]ost importantly ... is the Commission's power to conduct binding arbitration of a labor impasse. Given that we are currently in the eighth work stoppage in the past 22 seasons, it is unfortunate, but obvious, that baseball can not put its own house in order."[28] Continuing with the theme that intervention was necessary to resolve the dispute, Senator DeConcini, in the following excerpt, also defended government involving itself in the matter:

> Many people might wonder why, or if, Government should involve itself in this matter. But the Government is already involved and has, in effect, created a baseball monopoly.... This exemption allows baseball to operate as one large entity which operates free of the threat of competition, despite the fact that competition is the hallmark of American free enterprise. In other instances where we create a monopoly, such as utilities, no one questions the Government's authority to regulate the industry. In essence we grant the monopoly, but we do so with the understanding that this rare exception has conditions, one of which is the Government's right to regulate.[29]

While Senator DeConcini acknowledged that some thought Congress ought to repeal baseball's antitrust exemption, he "[thought] the larger issue [was] ... whether or not the game [could] ... police itself—I have not seen much recently to suggest that it can."[30]

H.R. 4994, Baseball Fans and Communities Protection Act of 1994 (103rd Congress)

Upon introducing H.R. 4994, Representative Mike Synar noted that it was "designed to spur the now stagnant negotiations between the players and owners of major league baseball. This bill is specifically designed to allow the players to get back to the field while all parties to the strike have their rights and bargaining positions protected through the application of the antitrust laws.... [G]iving the players antitrust remedies will preserve their bargaining [position] during the upcoming negotiations without having to resort to a strike."[31]

The committee report that accompanied the bill set forth the same reasoning, as shown by the following excerpt from the report:

> H.R. 4994 would subject Major League Baseball owners and players to the Nation's antitrust laws in the event one of those parties unilaterally imposes an anticompetitive term or condition on the other. While the case for a far broader repeal of the antitrust exemption is compelling, at this late juncture in the 103d Congress, the Committee opted to respond legislatively to the most urgent competitive problem facing Major League Baseball[:] its failure to be subject to the same antitrust rules as the other sports in the event of a breakdown of the collective bargaining process and the unilateral imposition of terms by one of the parties. As such, the legislation was specifically drafted so that it would not implicate issues relating to other activities, such as the operation of the minor leagues or franchise relocation.[32]
>
> The Committee's formal action of partially repealing the nonstatutory antitrust exemption which Congress never initiated or endorsed but by which it has been saddled for over 70 years is really the first step in ending a legal fiction about the game created and perpetuated by the Supreme Court, as perhaps one of its greatest indulgences. That indulgence, fueled first by sentimentality and then by risk-aversion, has now vested such complete power over the sport by its financial owners as to enable them to end the game at will.[33]
>
> The Committee now acts to end the illusion which has spawned very real economic consequences. It does so by partially repealing the nonstatutory exemption created by the 1922 decision in Federal Baseball Club of Baltimore v. National League of Professional Baseball Clubs. In so doing, the Committee responds to the current phase of a recurring crisis in baseball in a very limited, yet crucial, way: by subjecting the traditional parties to Major League Baseball's collective bargaining agreement the players union and owners to the Nation's antitrust laws in the event one party unilaterally imposes an anticompetitive term or condition of employment on the other.[34]

Other members of the Judiciary Committee disagreed, objecting to, among other things, congressional involvement in the matter. They wrote:

> We continue to be concerned about both the propriety and timing of this legislation and oppose its enactment. Simply put, Congress should not intervene in an ongoing collective bargaining dispute unless a national security interest is involved. Clearly, as important as baseball is to our national psyche, a baseball strike is not a national security matter. The

> decision to legislatively move ahead on this matter at this point is also highly questionable. It would make more sense for Congress to revisit the basic issue of baseball's antitrust exemption next year, when the emotion and acrimony surrounding the current strike hopefully will have subsided.[35]

The dissenting members of the committee also tackled the claim that the antitrust exemption served as a barrier to resolving the ongoing dispute between baseball players and owners. They noted that the other three professional sports leagues (basketball, football, and hockey) did not have the same antitrust exemption that baseball has, yet "all three ... have seen considerable labor strife, not dissimilar to that which we are witnessing with respect to baseball. It would appear that labor strife in professional sports has more to do with economics, than it has to do with the applicability of the federal antitrust laws."[36]

H.R. 5095, Major League Play Ball Act (103rd Congress)

A September 1994 hearing on H.R. 5095 offers some insight into how several members of the House Committee on Education and Labor, Subcommittee on Labor-Management Relations viewed the role of Congress in the strike. The following passages show that the chairman of the subcommittee, Representative Pat Williams, acknowledged, and concurred with, the committee's longstanding opposition to binding arbitration, but then explained why he chose to support congressional intervention in this instance:

> I want to tell our witnesses that you are appearing before a committee which has historically opposed binding arbitration. The Labor Committee is the committee that believes that collective bargaining works in America and should be allowed to continue unhampered by Federal intervention. That is my own belief, but this is baseball. However, for this committee to be encouraging binding arbitration is historic and virtually unprecedented.[37]

Representative Williams's comments at the hearing echoed the statement he made upon introducing the bill. An excerpt of the statement is as follows:

> This bill addresses the inability of the owners and players to collectively bargain effectively given the antitrust exemption for baseball.... Collective bargaining in this country works very well. Government should intervene in that process only at times of crises, and then only when it is clear that continued voluntary negotiations will not succeed.[38] My legislation is introduced in that spirit....[39]

Several other subcommittee members followed suit in supporting the use of binding arbitration to settle the strike. Similar to the chairman's approach, each of these other subcommittee members implied or suggested that collective bargaining is preferable, but that binding arbitration, or congressional intervention, is acceptable when parties are unable to reach an agreement.

Excerpts from Representative Donald M. Payne's, Representative Matthew G. Martinez's, and Representative Eliot L. Engel's statements, respectively, are as follows:

> I support the Chairman's initiative because I believe that collective bargaining is a positive tool in this country. The government should step in the picture when it is evident that continued voluntary negotiations are futile. If this bill [H.R. 5095] can alleviate some of the problems that resulted from the baseball strike this summer, then this legislation has my full support.[40] [Payne]
>
> Binding arbitration, I think, is one way to settle these things when there are disputes like that, and while I am a strong labor supporter, I have never really felt that even with labor that there are times when a third party shouldn't step in and see things in a reasonable, objective way when the negotiating parties can't.[41] [Martinez]
>
> I urge the parties to resolve their differences so that congressional intervention is not necessary, but I assure you that we will get involved in order to protect the interests of fans, local business owners, and, as they say, the best interests of baseball.[42] [Engel]

Another subcommittee member who supported this bill, Representative Major R. Owens, believed that the preferable, long-term solution was to repeal baseball's antitrust exemption. In the following excerpt, he provides his reasoning:

> While I fully support this bill, of course, it only provides a temporary solution to a long-term problem. The Congress really must take stronger action. Baseball's antitrust exemption has provided the owners with a monopoly through which players have been denied the rights enjoyed by employees in every other industry. Continuing Congress' past inaction on this issue would be tragic.... Since Justice Blackmun rendered that court's opinion [in 1922], baseball's antitrust exemption has paved the way for seven work stoppages to occur, and presented with a chance to act, Congress has balked each time. The season may be over, but the opportunity for Congress to act is not. I urge all Members, of course, to fully support this effort by

> Congressman Williams, but I think we should go further and I urge all Members of Congress to support the efforts going forward in the Judiciary Committee to finally cure this problem once and for all by taking away the antitrust exemption from baseball.[43]

Taking a different tack, other subcommittee members suggested that the baseball strike did not warrant congressional involvement, and that it should be resolved through collective bargaining. Excerpts from the statements of Representatives Peter Hoekstra, Steve Gunderson, and Harris W. Fawell, respectively, are as follows:

> I would encourage Congress at this point in time to stay out of this situation. I would encourage the witnesses to go back to the bargaining table to solve their problems. If we are going to get involved, we should wait until after this strike is solved, and we should not do anything in a short period of time. We have much more pressing problems to deal with.[44] [Hoekstra]
>
> As a Republican and a State legislator, I joined with the labor movement in Wisconsin to support binding arbitration, mandatory binding arbitration to eliminate the possibility of a work stoppage among the public schoolteachers in our State. I believe there was clearly a national interest or at least a State interest that required us to do that, and in that context we then had to look at an alternative to resolving the labor disputes. My question, very frankly, is to what degree and how do we determine whether there is a similar national interest with America's pastime, and if so, then what ought to be the conditions for an alternative remedy?... As I indicated earlier, I am not one who is philosophically opposed to the concept of binding public arbitration when there is an overriding public interest. My question to the players or to your representative is, because you seem to be the supporters of this legislation, what is the overriding public interest which would compel the United States Congress to order final and binding arbitration in this situation?[45] [Gunderson]
>
> I generally agree with the Chairman in not believing that we should mandate settlements. I think that probably as rough as this may be, it should be allowed to play out, and who knows what the next chapter of baseball may be. "[46] "I speak as somebody who has played ball all my life, I love the game, it is fascinating, but I don't believe in the final analysis it is an economic tragedy in this Nation.... I basically take the view that we ought not to break into this collective bargaining process as long as it is there. Antitrust laws are not involved anyway.... The strike has got to be settled, I believe, by the players, by the owners getting together and recognizing that each has some trust and some basis to their stands....[47] [Fawell]

At least two of the subcommittee members who supported the imposition of binding arbitration raised yet another issue: the possible financial impact of the strike on stadium or team employees. Representative Martinez stated that the work stoppage was "an economic disaster to the people who make a living from baseball.... [T]he people that sell the peanuts in the stands, the beer, and the people that work in the concessions...."[48] Echoing Representative Martinez's concern, Representative Engel noted that "[t]housands of people, many of them my constituents, rely on Major League Baseball for their livelihood. They are the ticket takers, hot dog vendors, and small business owners in the community...."[49]

Hearing on Baseball's Antitrust Exemption and the Strike (103rd Congress)

In September 1994, the House Committee on the Judiciary, Subcommittee on Economic and Commercial Law held a hearing on Major League Baseball's antitrust exemption and its relationship to the ongoing strike.[50]

As shown by the following passages, Representative Jack Brooks, chairman of the subcommittee, linked the two issues—baseball's antitrust exemption and the strike—and concluded that legislation was necessary.

> Now, Congress doesn't serve the function of mediator who shuttles between private parties to resolve individual disputes. But we are, however, policymakers, policymakers with a long memory.... They [the owners] may have shut it [baseball and the World Series, in particular] down for the first time since 1904, but you might be underestimating Congress' ability to respond to the debacle we have witnessed since August 12. They would be wise to remember there is a different rhythm to congressional deliberations and actions. The 406 games that have been lost, the 12.6 million people who have not enjoyed paying and going to a game have moved the issue of baseball's antitrust exemption to this committee's radar screen as never before.[51]
>
> As a result of the spectacle this Nation was forced to endure in the last few months and my very grave concerns for the future of the institution [baseball], I have come to the conclusion that legislation is needed to restore the principles of competition and fair play to the business of baseball. I am well aware that there may be insufficient time to pass a stand alone bill in the House before Congress adjourns, but I would remind the parties that the 104th Congress is schedule to convene well before spring training begins and well before the scheduled season opening on April 2. In addition, if before adjournment the Senate acts to attach a limited repeal of the exemption on

other legislation and sends it to the House, I would be very open to allowing it to proceed directly to the President.[52]

Expressing similar sentiments, Representative John Conyers Jr. said: "We are not negotiators. We are not bargainers, but we do make the law. We are responsible for our antitrust law. And it seems to me that unless something happens before the end—the beginning of the season next year, I think Congress is going to have a very heavy obligation to move in one of these directions...."[53]

Representative Patricia Schroeder, in the following excerpt, characterized Congress's lack of action regarding baseball's antitrust exemption as implicitly creating a link between Congress and major league baseball.

> I have seen the polls that the owners are circulating that tell us the public does not favor Congressional involvement in the current dispute between the players and the owners. I would suggest that each year that Congress allows the [antitrust] exemption to stand is another year of Congressional involvement. By doing nothing, we are allowing the owners a special entitlement.[54]

Offering another, yet related, perspective, Representative Sherwood Boehlert talked of Congress's responsibility for professional baseball. He said: "We believe that because of the unique station that baseball holds in American society, and because of the legal privileges it has been granted by Congress, we have a special responsibility to ensure that the game endures."[55]

Although Representative Brooks concluded the hearing by citing the need for legislation, he and at least two other subcommittee members (Representatives Conyers and Hamilton Fish Jr.) encouraged the heads of the players union and Major League Baseball—both of whom testified at the hearing—to resolve their differences through collective bargaining. Their comments (Brooks, Fish, and Conyers, respectively) were as follows:

> You know, we deal with problems all the time up here where I may have this position, somebody else has another position, and we are hard set in them and we are going to go with them. Yet very often in Congress people get together and realize that there are third and fourth positions and what you thought was such a wonderful idea really is not that significant, that important, and that you could have been wrong. I could have been wrong. We could have done something else, and we reach those alternatives often here. That is what compromise is, that is what politics is all about. That is what

negotiations are all about, and I would hope that you all would experience that opportunity. You have that opportunity any time.[56] [Brooks]

I don't think anybody has missed the fact that the chairman and I would very much like the parties here to resolve this dispute themselves and get on with the game.[57] [Fish]

Gentlemen, this has been an important hearing so far because it sounds like we might be able to get negotiations going again. I don't want to be overoptimistic, but I would certainly want to urge that if anything could come out of this hearing, the first thing that I think we would all rejoice about would be the fact that you were able to get back to the bargaining table, and I hope that could occur.[58] [Conyers]

H.R. 45, Baseball Fans and Communities Protection Act of 1995 (104th Congress)

In introducing H.R. 45, Representative Conyers identified baseball's antitrust exemption as being "at the root of the current strike," and suggested that Congress was in a position to intervene. Specifically, he said that "[w]e have the opportunity and ability to rescue the national pastime from its current dispiriting condition. Let's not allow this opportunity to pass by or be deferred. I urge all colleagues to join in the effort."[59]

H.R. 105, H.R. 106, H.R. 365, and H.R. 1612 (104th Congress)

In the absence of introductory statements or hearings, it is not known whether these bills were efforts to address the baseball strike, or reflect the Members' general interest in professional baseball. The bills and their titles and sponsors are as follows: H.R. 105, Baseball Antitrust Restoration Amendment of 1995, Representative Michael Bilirakis; H.R. 106,[60] Representative Michael Bilirakis; H.R. 365, Baseball Fans and Communities Protection Act of 1995, Representative Charles Schumer; and, H.R. 1612, Major League Baseball Antitrust Reform Act of 1995, Representative Jim Bunning.

H.R. 120, Baseball Fans and Communities Protection Act of 1995 (104th Congress)

Although he did not mention his bill specifically, Representative Bunning stated that "[m]ajor league baseball has to have this exemption removed for the good of the fans, the game, and anybody else that wants a season in 1995."[61]

H.R. 386, Professional Baseball Antitrust Reform Act of 1995 (104th Congress)

Similar to other Members who believed that the antitrust exemption was at the root of the strike, Representative James A. Traficant Jr. believed that "[r]emoving this [antitrust] exemption may be the only way to end the strike and save the 1995 season. That's why today I am introducing the Professional Baseball Antitrust Reform Act of 1995."[62]

H.R. 397, Major League Play Ball Act (104th Congress)

While proposing a partial, or complete, repeal of baseball's antitrust exemption was a relatively common response to the strike, Representative Pat Williams, in the following excerpt, recommended binding arbitration: "I have today introduced legislation to provide mandatory and binding arbitration if the parties fail to reach agreement. Collective bargaining in this country works very well. The public, through their government, should intervene only in a crisis. We now have reached a crisis in the well-being of our national pastime."[63]

H.R. 735, National Commission on Professional Baseball Act of 1995 (104th Congress)

Representative John J. LaFalce, in discussing the rationale for his bill, noted that someone (that is, Congress) needed to protect the fans' interests, and proposed that regulating baseball was one way to do this. Excerpts from Representative LaFalce's statement are as follows:

> It is clear that baseball owners and players will continue to look out only for their own needs. But there is a crying need for someone to look out for the interests of fans, of taxpayers and of the communities in which both major league and minor league baseball is played. It is time for Congress to take steps to return baseball to the American people. The legislation I am introducing today seeks to accomplish this by creating an independent National Commission on Professional Baseball. The Commission would serve as a temporary regulatory body and impartial arbitrator to oversee the conduct of professional baseball until the legal status of major league baseball can be redefined either by negotiation or by congressional legislation.[64]
>
> My legislation does take the position that baseball's antitrust exemption is, in effect, a government-granted monopoly in much the same manner as a local public utility or transportation authority. And like any other publicly-sanctioned monopoly, my bill would require public oversight to assure that

> self-interest is not put above the interests of the public and consumers. In this regard, the proposed commission would be similar to the Federal Communications Commission, or any other public body with oversight over a restricted industry or market. An important difference, however is the fact that the authority of the proposed Commission is intended to be temporary during a period of deregulation of baseball from the current market restrictions imposed by baseball's current antitrust exemption. Since Federal law has permitted a restricted national market for major league baseball, the Federal Government has both the right and the responsibility to regulate this market, just as we regulate other monopolies, to assure that the public's interests are protected.[65]

H.R. 749[66] (104th Congress)

Advocating an approach also favored by several of his colleagues, Representative Estaban Edward Torres introduced legislation to repeal baseball's antitrust exemption. He provided the following reasons for doing so: "For the short term, I believe repealing the antitrust exemption will accelerate the end of the baseball shutdown, which threatens the livelihoods of thousands of Americans and the economies of cities and towns across the country. For the long term, I believe repealing the antitrust exemption will restore fairness to the fragile relationship of labor and management in professional baseball."[67]

H.R. 870 and S. 376, Major League Baseball Restoration Act (104th Congress)

As discussed below, President Clinton forwarded proposed legislation to Congress in 1995. His proposal became H.R. 870, which was introduced by Representative Pat Williams, and S. 376, which was introduced by Senator Edward M. Kennedy.

After noting that Congress generally prefers to let parties involved in labor disputes reach a settlement on their own, Senator Kennedy offered several reasons why it was desirable for Congress to intervene in the baseball strike. In the following excerpts from his remarks, he touched on Congress's authority to regulate interstate commerce and the special status of baseball in America.

> Generally, Congress is reluctant to inject itself in labor disputes. All of us hope that the parties will find a way to end the impasse and settle their differences voluntarily. But there are rare instances in which Congress has a role to play in settling such disputes, and this may well be one of those times.

> There is no doubt that Congress' constitutional authority to regulate interstate commerce gives us the power to enact legislation to settle this dispute. Many aspects of major league baseball affect commerce between the States....
>
> Obviously, Congress does not intervene in every labor dispute that burdens interstate commerce, but baseball is different and unique. It is more than a nationwide industry. It is our national sport. Baseball is part of American life.
>
> We in Congress as representatives of fans throughout the country should not remain silent while baseball is damaged by a strike that the owners and players seem unable to resolve themselves. Clearly, Congress has the power to act. The question is who speaks for Red Sox and millions of other fans across America. At this stage in the deadlock, if Congress does not speak for them, it may well be that no one will.
>
> For all these reasons, Congress can act and should be prepared to act. Legislation to end the strike would not set a precedent for injecting Congress into other labor disputes. There is still time for the owners and players to resolve this dispute on their own or to act voluntarily to establish a safety mechanism for doing so.[68]

S. 15, National Pastime Preservation Act of 1995 (104th Congress)

S. 15 was yet another bill that, if enacted, would have repealed baseball's antitrust exemption. Its sponsor, Senator Daniel Patrick Moynihan, made the following remarks when he introduced the bill:

> As a result of this anomaly [baseball's antitrust exemption] in American law, Mr. President, the World Series was cancelled in 1994 for the first time since 1904. With none of the legal restraints that prevent other businesses from engaging in anticompetitive behavior, the baseball team owners are free to act as a cartel. To end this monopoly, Congress must remove baseball's antitrust exemption and subject the game to the same rules of law that apply to all other major league sports.... Many Members of Congress have begun to examine this issue more closely in view of the strike. My Friend Senator ORRIN HATCH, the new chairman of the Judiciary Committee, has indicated that he supports repealing the exemption and is prepared to move a bill quickly through his committee.[69]

S. 415, Professional Baseball Antitrust Reform Act of 1995, and S. 416, Major League Baseball Antitrust Reform Act of 1995[70] (104th Congress)

In February 1995, the Senate Committee on the Judiciary, Subcommittee on Antitrust, Business Rights, and Competition held a hearing on baseball's antitrust exemption and two bills, S. 415 and S. 416, that would apply antitrust laws to professional baseball. At the hearing, several Members offered diverse views regarding whether the proposed repeal of baseball's antitrust exemption ought to be linked to the strike and the desirability of congressional intervention in the strike.

Senator Strom Thurmond, who introduced S. 416, did not link the partial, or complete, repeal of baseball's antitrust exemption to the ongoing strike. The following are excerpts from his remarks:

> The Thurmond-Leahy legislation addresses baseball's antitrust exemption, but is not specially drafted in an attempt to solve the current baseball strike.... Some Members of Congress believe that we should not get involved during the current strike, while other Members have asserted that in the absence of a strike there is no need for the Congress to take action on this issue. Whether there is a strike or not, it is my belief that it is proper for the Congress to consider this antitrust issue as a matter of public policy.[71]

Regarding the purpose of the February 1995 hearing, Senator Thurmond said that it was "intended to focus on the policy implications of baseball's antitrust exemption, rather than the details of the current baseball strike and the course of the unsuccessful negotiations. Although the ongoing strike raises questions about the antitrust exemption, the problems in major league baseball go deeper than this one strike."[72] Senator Thurmond added that he "intend[ed] to continue working on this issue, even if the strike were to end today."[73]

Senator Thurmond also shared his thoughts on the circumstances under which it might be acceptable for government to intervene in a matter such as the baseball strike, indicating it depended upon whether the public interest would be served. In the following passage, the Senator also commented on Congress's implicit involvement in baseball's antitrust exemption.

> Despite our interest in seeing the players return to the field, we must be ever mindful of the need to limit Federal Government intervention into matters best left to private remedies. The Congress should determine how much Federal involvement, if any, serves the public interest in this area. But as long as the special antitrust exemption remains in place for baseball, the Congress is involved. The Congress has an impact on the sport by simply permitting the special exemption to remain long after the factual basis for it has disappeared.[74]

Senator Orrin G. Hatch, who introduced S. 415, was one of several subcommittee members that linked the ongoing baseball strike to professional baseball's antitrust exemption, and, accordingly, supported eliminating the exemption. Senator Hatch's comments were as follows:

> Unlike other legislation that has been proposed, my bill would not impose a big-government solution. On the contrary, it would get government out of the way by eliminating a serious Government-made obstacle [baseball's antitrust exemption] to settlement....
>
> A limited repeal of this antitrust immunity is now in order. Labor negotiations between owners and players are impeded by the fact that baseball players, unlike all other workers, have no resort under the law if the baseball owners act in a manner that would, in the absence of the immunity, violate the antitrust laws. This aberration in the antitrust laws has handed the owners a huge club that gives them unique leverage in bargaining and discourages them from accepting reasonable terms. This is an aberration that Government has created, and it is an aberration that Government should fix....
>
> This legislation would not impose any terms of settlement on the disputing parties, nor would it require that they reach a settlement. Rather, it would simply remove a serious impediment to settlement—an impediment that is the product of an aberration in our antitrust laws. In short, far from involving any governmental intrusion into the pending baseball dispute, the legislation would get Government out of the way.[75]

Although Senator Patrick Leahy was Senator Thurmond's cosponsor, he is one of the Members who asserted that the antitrust exemption played a role in the strike. However, he also identified, in the following comments, two other factors that he asserted contributed to the ongoing dispute.

> There is a public interest in the resumption of true, major league baseball. The current situation derives at least in part from circumstances in which the Federal antitrust laws have not applied, Congress has provided no regulatory framework to protect the public, and the major leagues have chosen to operate without a strong, independent commissioner who could look out for the best interest of baseball. Thus, competing financial interests continue to clash, with no resolution in sight.[76]

Senator Daniel Patrick Moynihan, although an original cosponsor of S. 415, favored resolution of the labor-management dispute through collective agreement. Excerpts from his remarks are as follows:

> Clearly baseball is a business engaged in interstate commerce, and should be subject to the antitrust laws to the same extent that all other businesses are. But the greater point is that the strike must be settled through good-faith bargaining between the parties. I will support this and any other effort that will move the parties forward toward a collective bargaining agreement—and the resumption of baseball in America as soon as possible.[77]
>
> As a former Assistant Secretary of Labor under Presidents Kennedy and Johnson, I agree with Senator Hatch, Senator Kassebaum, and others who have said Congress ought not interfere in the collective bargaining process—in baseball or any other industry. Absent some compelling national interest, Congress has always been reluctant to intervene in labor disputes, and properly so. Yet by our *inaction* with regard to the antitrust exemption, we *have* been interfering with baseball for half a century.[78]

Other members of the subcommittee offered reasons why Congress should refrain from intervening in the strike. Senator Arlen Specter simply stated that he did not "think that the Congress ought to intervene when a dispute is in process, and certainly not to order binding arbitration."[79] Senator Howell Heflin, who said he had "great reservations about Congress intervening in any labor dispute," described two of them in the following passage:

> Reservations, No. 1, as to whether or not we are equipped to be the decisionmaker and whether we ought to take action which might be favorable or unfavorable to one side or the other. I have also questions as to whether or not in any labor dispute anything other than the economic pressures that come to bear should have a substantial interest or controlling interest in the determination of the settlement of the dispute or the terms that come up. On the other hand, I want to see baseball played. I want to see the fans' interest in it gratified.[80]

Raising questions regarding, for example, Congress's priorities and the expected effectiveness of the proposed legislation, Senator Nancy Landon Kassebaum said the following:

> At the outset, let me say that I believe it would be a mistake for Congress to intervene in the current dispute between the Major League Baseball owners and players. It is not the role of Congress—absent a national emergency—to force a settlement or take sides in a private labor dispute. To make an exception in this case would establish a very dangerous precedent.... Let me outline briefly my three principal objections to the Hatch-Moynihan bill.

First, the Hatch-Moynihan bill [S. 415]—by its own terms—would be a direct intervention by Congress in the current baseball labor dispute.... Again, I believe it is a mistake for us to intervene by changing the rules in the middle of the game.

Second, not only would Hatch-Moynihan intervene in the current dispute, it would, worse still, take sides.... Hatch-Moynihan would treat the baseball owners less favorably than any other industry by excluding baseball's collective bargaining process from federal antitrust laws. This would allow the players to take the dispute to court, a right nonlabor organization now enjoys....

Finally, it is my view that consideration of this or any legislation, at this time, will only impede further negotiations and decrease the likelihood of a settlement. As long as one side or the other believes there is a possibility that Congress will step in, meaningful negotiations will not occur.[81]

S. 627, Major League Baseball Antitrust Reform Act of 1995 (104th Congress)

Having introduced S. 415 previously, Senator Hatch, along with four colleagues, including Senator Thurmond, introduced a new bill, S. 627, in March 1995. Senator Hatch's and Senator Thurmond's positions remained unchanged regarding whether the purpose of the legislation was to facilitate the resolution of the strike (Hatch's position), or to terminate Congress's connection to baseball's antitrust exemption (Thurmond's position).[82]

During a hearing on S. 627, several members of the Senate Committee on the Judiciary provided a variety of reasons why Congress ought not to intervene in the strike. Questions about congressional priorities, the potential for legislation to disrupt collective bargaining efforts, and concern that congressional action would be viewed as favoring one party to the dispute over the other were put forth as reasons for Congress not to act. Senator Specter's, Senator Paul Simon's, and Senators Hank Brown and Dianne Feinstein's comments were as follows, respectively:

Whatever the merits of eliminating major league baseball's broad, judicially created exemption from the antitrust laws, Congress should not act while the labor situation remains uncertain. Any action we take is certain to be viewed as favoring one side to the dispute or the other. In such instances, Congress acts best when it does not act at all. The complex labor problems that have characterized baseball for the past years ought to be resolved by the parties without congressional interference.... Whether or not that [baseball's] exemption ought to be retained, I believe strongly that given the current state of play, it would be a mistake for Congress to enact this bill. This bill would only upset the current situation, making it less likely that the parties to baseball's labor strife will be able to resolve their dispute between themselves. We should not lose sight of the fact that voluntary collective bargaining is the basis of labor relations in this country. The parties should be left to settle their current impasse themselves without interference from Congress.[83] [Specter]

In approving a repeal of major league baseball's longstanding antitrust exemption, this Committee has decided to alter the balance of power in an ongoing labor dispute between millionaires while the truly pressing problems facing our nation remain unresolved. Congress should be devoting its time and resources to other matters rather than inserting itself into a controversy for which both sides deserve blame. Indeed, of the many labor disputes ongoing in America today, I can think of few, if any, that are less deserving of our attention than this one.... The variety of problems facing our professional sports leagues demonstrates that even if professional baseball is a deserving subject of Congress's attention, such consideration should not take place on an *ad hoc* basis, in response to one 'crisis' or another, but should be part of an overall and careful reexamination of professional sports under the law. Only by studying the issue raised by S. 627 in this broader context can Congress avoid the justifiable criticism that it is simply playing favorites in a rancorous dispute that, but for the parties' stubbornness and lack of reason, should have been resolved long ago.[84] [Simon]

The current bill intervenes in a continuing labor dispute. The majority report justifies this legislation on the basis that it 'would help resolve baseball's labor problems.' This conclusion is dubious at best. The middle of an ongoing labor dispute is not the right time to change the rules of the game. Both President Clinton and his chosen mediator, William Usery, repeatedly stated that the problems of baseball should be decided at the negotiating table. But, every time this issue comes before Congress, the parties drop what they are doing, leave the negotiating table, and focus their efforts on legislation.[85] Proponents of the legislation suggest that all of the labor discord in Baseball can somehow be attributed to the existence of the exemption and that its elimination would be a labor panacea. Nothing could be further from the truth. In fact, all that its elimination would cause is unbridled litigation.[86] [Brown and Feinstein]

White House Efforts to Aid in Resolving the Strike

On October 14, 1994, the Secretary of Labor, Robert Reich, announced that former Labor Secretary William Usery had "agreed to mediate the labor dispute between Major League Baseball players and owners. And the players and owners have agreed to resume negotiations with Bill Usery as special mediator."[87]

On January 26, 1995, President Clinton issued a statement, saying that he had asked Mr. Usery "to bring the owners and the players back to the table, and to step up the pace and intensity of his mediation efforts. I have asked him to report back to me by February 6 with the progress they have made." While the President said that "[i]t has always been my belief—and continues to be—that the baseball strike, like any labor dispute, should be settled through good-faith bargaining between the parties," he added "[b]ut we cannot wait indefinitely."[88]

On February 7, 1995, President Clinton "summoned the two sides to the White House ... for a last-ditch negotiating session," which, ultimately, was unsuccessful.[89] Speaking in the briefing room at the White House shortly before 11:00 p.m. on February 7, President Clinton provided the following update:

> Clearly they are not capable of settling this strike without an umpire. So I have now concluded, since I have no legal authority in this situation, as all of you know and have known for some time, that I should send to the Congress legislation seeking binding arbitration of the baseball dispute. This is not a request for a congressionally imposed solution. It is a request for the only process we have left to us to find a solution through neutral parties.[90]

After acknowledging that Congress has "other pressing business," the President added, "[a]t least when the bill [I propose] goes to the Congress, the American people can make themselves heard one way or the other on the legislation and Congress can consider it."[91]

The next day, President Clinton transmitted proposed legislation, "Major League Baseball Restoration Act," to Congress. As discussed above, Representative Williams and Senator Kennedy introduced the bill in the House of Representatives (H.R. 870) and the Senate (S. 376), respectively. The President's rationale for proposing legislation included the following reasons: "If the dispute is permitted to continue, there is likely to be substantial economic damage to the cities and communities in which major league franchises are located and to the communities that host spring training. The ongoing dispute also threatens further serious harm to an important national institution."[92]

Discussion

As measured by the number of legislative measures introduced and hearings held, and as shown in **Table 8**, Congress was most active during the 1994 strike. The 232-day baseball strike lasted much longer than the two NFL strikes and included the loss of the 1994 World Series. The 1982 and 1987 strikes were relatively short by comparison, lasting 57 days and 24 days, respectively. Although the 1987 strike involved the use of replacement players for several games during the regular season, the season was capped by the Super Bowl. The 1982 Super Bowl also was held.

Table 9 organizes the legislative measures according to the method proposed for resolving the dispute. S. 3003 (97th Congress) is included in two columns (impose binding arbitration and require league and players to resume activities) because it included two noteworthy provisions.

Three methods were proposed for ending the 1982 or 1987 NFL strikes—impose binding arbitration, encourage the parties to reconcile their differences, or require the league and players to resume normal activities (that is, resume playing games). Neither of the latter two options was proposed for baseball. Major league baseball enjoys a unique status as the only professional sport in the United States that has a broad antitrust exemption, and fifteen legislative measures targeted the exemption, attempting to eliminate or modify it. Four measures were introduced that would have imposed binding arbitration on baseball; two measures would have established a commission to oversee baseball; and one measure would have amended the Sports Broadcasting Act regarding professional baseball.

The following table shows the disposition of the legislative measures introduced or offered in response to the 1982 NFL strike, the 1987 NFL strike, or the 1994 MLB strike.

Table 8. Congressional Activity During Strikes

	1982 NFL Strike	1987 NFL Strike	1994 MLB Strike
Legislative Measure(s)	3	1	22[a]
Hearing(s)	0	0	5

Source: Legislative Information System, at http://www.congress.gov.

Notes:

a. As discussed above, it is uncertain whether H.R. 105, H.R. 106, H.R. 365, and H.R. 1612, which are included here, were related to the 1994 MLB strike.

Table 9. Methods Proposed for Resolving the Strikes

Support Reconciliation (Congress)	Establish a Commission (Congress)	Impose Binding Arbitration (Congress)	Eliminate or Modify MLB's Antitrust Exemption (Congress)	Amend the Sports Broadcasting Act (Congress)	Require League and Players to Resume Activities (Congress)
H.Res. 597 (97th)	S. 2401 (103rd)	S. 3003 (97th)[a]	S. 2380 (103rd)	H.R. 105 (104th)[b]	S. 3 003 (97th)[a,c]
H.Res. 598 (97th)	H.R. 735 (104th)	H.R. 5095 (103rd)	S.Amdt. 2601 to H.R. 4649 (103rd)		
S.Res. 294 (100th)		H.R. 397 (104th)	H.R. 4965 (103rd)		
		Y.R. 870 (104th)			
		S. 376 (104th)	H.R. 4994 (103rd)		
			H.R. 45 (104th)		
			H.R. 106[b] (104th)		
			H.R. 120 (104th)		
			H.R. 365[b] (104th)		
			H.R. 386 (104th)		
			H.R. 749 (104th)		
			H.R. 1612[b] (104th)		
			S. 15 (104th)		
			S. 415 (104th)		
			S. 416 (104th)		
			S. 627 (104th)		

Source: Legislative Information System, at http://www.congress.gov. Notes:
a. This bill is included in two columns.

b. As discussed above, it is uncertain whether H.R. 105, H.R. 106, H.R. 365, and H.R. 1612 were related to the 1994 MLB strike.

c. While urging the NFL and the NFLPA to "take all necessary steps to resume activities," S. 3003 would have directed them to return to the "status quo" that existed "prior to 12:01 antemeridian [morning] of September 21, 1982," which, in effect would have required that games be resumed. (Sec. 3 of S. 3003 (97th Congress).) The final game played before the strike began took place Monday night, Sept. 20, 1982, between the Green Bay Packers and the New York Giants. Hence, the language in S. 3003 refers to the status quo of the regular season. (Len Pasquarelli, "Lengthy Strike Has Mostly Been Forgotten," *ESPN.com*, Sept. 21, 2007, at http://sports.espn.go.com/nfl/columns/story?columnist=pasquarelli_len&id=3030311.

Table 10. Disposition of Legislative Measures

Withdrawn (Congress)	Not Reported by Committee[a] (Congress)	Placed on Senate or House Calendar (Congress)	Agreed to by Voice Vote (Congress)
S.Amdt. 2601 to H.R.	H.Res. 597 (97th)	S. 2380 (103rd)	S.Res. 294 (100th)
4649 (103rd)	H.Res. 598 (97th)	H.R. 4994 (103rd)	
	S. 3003 (97th)	S. 376 (104th)	
	H.R. 4965 (103rd)	S. 627 (104th)	
	S. 2401 (103rd)		
	H.R. 5095 (103rd)		
	H.R. 45 (104th)		
	H.R. 105 (104th) [b]		
	H.R. 106 (104th) [b]		
	H.R. 120 (104th)		
	H.R. 365 (104th) [b]		
	H.R. 386 (104th)		
	H.R. 397 (104th)		
	H.R. 735 (104th)		
	H.R. 749 (104th)		
	H.R. 870 (104th)		
	H.R. 1612 (104th) [b]		
	S. 15 (104th)		
	S. 415 (104th)		
	S. 416 (104th)		

Source: Legislative Information System, at http://www.congress.gov. Notes:

a. These are bills that were referred to a committee, but were not reported by the committee. See **Table 5**, **Table 6**, and **Table 7**.

b. As discussed above, it is uncertain whether H.R. 105, H.R. 106, H.R. 365, and H.R. 1612 were related to the 1994 MLB strike.

Among the 26 legislative measures introduced, the only one that was approved was S.Res. 294 (100th Congress), which encouraged NFL players and management to return to the bargaining table. Four bills, all related to the 1994 baseball strike, were placed on a Senate or House calendar. The one amendment (S.Amdt. 2601 to H.R. 4649 (103rd Congress)) that was offered was withdrawn. Most of the measures (20) were not reported by committee.

APPENDIX A. SUMMARY OF NFL LABOR HISTORY[93]

Chronology

1982	"The NFLPA's request to team owners to receive 55 percent of league revenue is denied, prompting a 57-day strike. The PA [players association] gains little."
1987	"NFL players vote to strike and owners field replacement players, After only 24 days, the players end their strike with no appreciable gains earned. The union files suit against the NFL, claiming that labor laws and collective bargaining, as conducted by the league, aren't working for the benefit of its players. A judge agrees, and in 1989, the Plan B limited system of free agency begins."
1989	"A federal appeals court reverses the 1987 court decision, claiming that antitrust laws do not apply because the NFLPA is a labor union. NFLPA Executive Director Gene Upshaw immediately decertifies the union."
1992	"Players win the right to free agency in the Freeman McNeil antitrust case, clearing the way for new collective-bargaining agreement negotiations."
1993	"The NFLPA is recertified as a union, the final step necessary before signing a new CBA. The new agreement establishes the league's first year of free agency and its first salary cap, which is set at $35 million. That cap will subsequently rise; for the 2009 season, it is projected to be $123 million."
2005	"The salary cap increases to $85.5 million, boosted by the opening of five new stadiums and three extensive renovations since the last extension of the CBA, in 2002."
2006	"NFL owners vote 30-2 to accept the NFLPA's proposal to extend the CBA, a deal that gives the players approximately 60 percent of total football revenue."

2009 "Owners in May vote 32-0 to opt out of the CBA they agreed to extend in 2006."

APPENDIX B. SPORTS AND LABOR-MANAGEMENT RELATIONS[94]

The National Labor Relations Act (NLRA)[95] governs labor-management relations in the private sector and applies generally to professional sports employers. Under the NLRA, employers and unions are required to bargain in good faith with respect to wages, hours, and other terms and conditions of employment.[96] Employers and unions are required to bargain over these mandatory subjects of bargaining to the point of impasse. The NLRA does not obligate either party, however, to agree to a proposal or to make a concession.[97] In fact, collective bargaining presupposes the availability of certain economic weapons as part of the negotiating process.[98] For example, employees are permitted to strike if collective bargaining fails to achieve higher wages or improved working conditions.[99] Similarly, during certain work stoppages, an employer may use replacement workers to continue the operation of its business.

Although the NLRA contemplates possible strikes by employees, it does provide for mediation and conciliation services to settle certain disputes. The NLRA authorizes the Federal Mediation and Conciliation Service (FMCS) to provide mediation and conciliation services upon its own motion or upon the request of one or more of the parties to a dispute whenever "in its judgment such dispute threatens to cause a substantial interruption of commerce."[100] The FMCS is directed, however, to avoid mediating disputes that would have only a minor effect on interstate commerce, if state or other conciliation services are available to the parties.[101] Where the FMCS is involved in a dispute, it is limited to providing only mediation and conciliation services, and may not issue a binding arbitration decision.

As noted earlier in this chapter, numerous measures were introduced in Congress in 1982 and 1994 to prescribe binding arbitration to resolve the NFL and MLB strikes. In general, these measures would have established a board or panel to take testimony, conduct hearings, and review relevant books and records. The board or panel would then consider various factors in conjunction with the information it received before rendering a final decision or agreement that would bind the parties and replace the expired collective bargaining agreement. Some of the factors that would have been considered include the history of collective bargaining agreements between the parties, the changes in circumstances of the parties, and an owner's ability to pay. [102] Unlike current legislation, such as the Employee Free Choice Act,[103] that would amend the NLRA to prescribe binding arbitration if certain conditions are not met in any private labor negotiation, many of the NFL and MLB measures would have established a panel or board to resolve a specific strike. It appears that the panel or board would have ceased to operate once a decision was reached.

Arbitration is often favored by disputing parties because it allows generally for the selection of arbitrators who have expertise in the industry in which the dispute arises.[104] Unlike judges who may or may not be familiar with certain industry concepts, arbitrators may be people who have worked as officials or regulators in the relevant community.[105] Indeed, at least one of the MLB measures would have established an arbitration board consisting of one representative of the owners of major league baseball selected by the owners, one representative of the major league baseball player's association selected by the association, and a third individual selected in accordance with the procedures of the American Arbitration Association or procedures otherwise agreed to by the parties.[106]

Supporters of arbitration have also maintained that it provides for faster dispute resolution because it is not subject generally to the rules and procedures that exist with litigation. Increasingly, however, the use of lawyers is becoming more common in arbitration. Consequently, whether arbitration is really a cost-effective alternative to litigation has been questioned. It has also been noted that arbitration fees may be costly.

APPENDIX C. ANTITRUST EXEMPTIONS APPLICABLE TO PROFESSIONAL SPORTS[107]

There is one statutory exemption from the antitrust laws applicable generally to professional sports, the Sports Broadcasting Act,[108] and two non-statutory exemptions: the so-called "baseball antitrust exemption" describes the fact that major league baseball, alone among professional sports, is not covered by the antitrust laws;[109] the judicially created labor-antitrust exemption is utilized by all professional sports leagues inasmuch as it is applicable to the collective bargaining agreements between players and their teams. Each will be briefly summarized in the following paragraphs, after which an element in many, if not most, professional team-sports contracts—the "reserve" clause[110]—will be noted and briefly discussed. Finally, there will be a short section on the 1998 congressional attempt to limit the "baseball antitrust exemption." Further, or more specific, information may be obtained directly from the author(s).

Sports Broadcasting Act (SBA)

The SBA's five sections include the following:

The first section of the act (15 U.S.C. § 1291) authorizes professional sports teams (including football teams) to pool, by "joint agreement," their broadcasting ("sponsored telecasting")[111] rights in their games in order that their leagues may sell or transfer those rights; and specifically makes the federal antitrust laws inapplicable to such joint agreements and sales or transfers.[112] (In 1988, the U.S. Court of Appeals for the Second Circuit ruled that the provision does not limit the antitrust exemption to a single, pooled-rights contract with a single television network.[113])

15 U.S.C. § 1292 clarifies that the antitrust exemption granted in § 1291 does not apply to contracts for the sale of telecasting rights that seek to limit the buyer's right to telecast games into *any* territory, except that a league may prohibit the telecasting of games into the home territory of any team when that team is playing a home game.[114]

The other three sections of the SBA (1) carve out Friday evenings (after 6 o'clock) and all day Saturdays between the second Friday in September and the second Saturday in December for high school and college games by specifically noting that the antitrust exemption provided in § 1291 does not apply to contracts that permit the telecasts of professional games during those times *if* the high school or college games were announced prior to August 1 of the applicable year as "regularly scheduled for such day and place" (§ 1293); (2) clarify that with the exception of the exemption granted in § 1291, the applicability of the antitrust laws to "organized professional team sports" remains unchanged (§ 1294); and (3) define "persons" as meaning individuals, partnerships, corporations, or "unincorporated association[s][115] or any combination" of them (§ 1295).

"Baseball Antitrust Exemption"

The so-called "baseball antitrust exemption"—a convenient and much-used shorthand phrase—is, technically, not accurate because it implies positive action by Congress to grant an exemption. In fact, the "exemption" is the result of an historical accident: the first case to come before the Supreme Court alleging a violation of the antitrust laws occurred prior to the Supreme Court's expansive interpretation of the Commerce Clause. In that case, the Court held that the business of putting on "exhibitions of baseball" could not be considered commerce for purposes of federal antitrust jurisdiction;[116] and although the Court has had several opportunities to reverse its position that the antitrust laws are not applicable to professional baseball, it has never done so, preferring that the change be made specifically by Congress.[117]

While the fact of an antitrust exemption for professional baseball has been recognized since 1922, the *extent* and *scope* of that exemption, however, has been the subject of some lower court discussion. At least one court has interpreted the Supreme Court's holdings and language as limiting the exemption to baseball's "reserve system," noted, *infra,* pursuant to which player movement from team to team may be restrained.

Labor-Antitrust Exemption

The judicially created labor-antitrust exemption holds that Congress's desire to foster collective bargaining is best furthered by permitting employees who wish to jointly negotiate the terms of their employment contracts to do so without fear of violating the antitrust laws. The exemption is not completely open-ended, however, specifying that the practices negotiated must (1) inherently constitute mandatory subjects of collective bargaining (i.e., be bona fide terms or conditions of employment); (2) be no more restrictive than necessary to realize the goal(s) it/they purport(s) to achieve; and (3) be embodied in a valid, genuinely negotiated (i.e., arm's-length) collective bargaining agreement. In addition, some courts have indicated that another factor to be evaluated is whether the restraint embodied in the agreement affects only or primarily the parties to the agreement (as opposed to competitors of either).[118] If the labor-antitrust doctrine is applicable, it covers the management as well as labor parties to a collective bargaining agreement. As the Supreme Court explained in *Connell Construction Co. v. Plumbers & Steamfitters Local Union No. 100,*

> The nonstatutory exemption has its source in the strong labor policy favoring the association of employees to eliminate competition over wages and working conditions. Union success in organizing workers and standardizing wages ultimately will affect price competition among employers, but the goals of federal labor law could never be achieved if this effect on business competition were held a violation of the antitrust laws. The Court therefore has acknowledged that labor policy requires tolerance for the lessening of business competition based on differences in wages and working conditions.[119]

The "Reserve" Clause in Professional Sports; Congress's Attempt to Address the Issue in the Context of the "Baseball Antitrust Exemption"

Under most circumstances, the value of an offered service (e.g., the services of a professional athlete) would be determined by the market. Prospective buyers of that service would bid on it and bargain with the seller, who, if he has an especially unique or valuable commodity to sell, would profit from his ability to exploit the competition among potential buyers. Once a professional athlete is under contract to a sports team, however, the "reserve" clause in professional sports prohibits that interplay among market participants by, in essence, binding the athlete to the team that has him under contract—at least in the year following the contract's expiration. The argument that "the restriction of competition for players' services is not a type of restraint proscribed by the Sherman Act" has been made and rejected.[120]

But that same court would not dismiss the utility of the NFL's "Rozelle" rule, noting that the "'ostensible purposes' of the rule are to maintain competitive balance among ... teams and protect the clubs' investment in scouting, selecting and developing players."[121] Even the district court hearing the relatively recent challenge to baseball's "reserve" clause observed:

> Clearly the preponderance of credible proof does not favor elimination of the reserve clause. With the sole exception of plaintiff [Curt Flood] himself, it shows that even plaintiff's witnesses do not contend that it is wholly undesirable; in fact they regard substantial portions meritorious....[122]

Thus, the various "reserve" clauses have not been struck down completely; they have, however, been modified to conform to judicial criticism of their enforcement and/or lack of bona fide bargaining—most "reserve" clauses are simply imported from the Leagues' Constitutions and Bylaws and inserted in their Standard Player Contracts.

In the years after the Supreme Court's *Flood* decision[123] refusing to alter or remove baseball's antitrust exemption, Congress had made several attempts to act on the Court's invitation in that case to correct the historical accident of baseball's antitrust exemption,[124] but none was successful until the passage of the Curt Flood Act by the 105th Congress.[125] The Curt Flood Act is applicable to major league baseball players,[126] clarifying that they are covered by the antitrust laws in transactions concerning their employment to the same extent as are other professional athletes.[127] Among the issues specifically not covered or affected (in addition to employment relations with minor league players) is "the agreement [known as the "Professional Baseball Agreement"] between organized professional major league baseball teams and the National Association of Professional Baseball Leagues."

We are not aware of any litigation brought pursuant to the Curt Flood Act: although the act does get major league professional baseball players past the courthouse door by denying their employers the "we're-not-covered-by-the-antitrust-laws-so-this-case-must-be-dismissed" argument, as the foregoing material has indicated. Once in court many professional athletes have been frustrated in their attempts to challenge practices they consider onerous if those practices are embodied in valid collective bargaining agreements. The Curt Flood Act neither prevents the courts from recognizing the nonstatutory labor-antitrust exemption, nor provides guidance on the interpretation of that exemption.

End Notes

1 National Football League, NFL Management Council and NFL Players Association, *NFL Collective Bargaining Agreement 2006-2012*, March 8, 2006, p. 240. A "league year" is "the period from March 1 of one year through and including the last day of February of the following year, or such other one year period to which the NFL and the NFLPA may agree." (Ibid., p. 4.)

2 Ibid., p. 240. (Boldface and italics in original.) "'Capped Year' means any League Year for which a Salary Cap is in effect." (Ibid., p. 6.) "'Salary Cap' means the absolute maximum amount of Salary that each Club may pay or be obligated to pay or provide to players or Player Affiliates, or may pay or be obligated to pay to third parties at the request of and for the benefit of Players or Player Affiliates, at any time during a particular League Year, in accordance with the Rules set forth in Article XXIV (Guaranteed League-wide Salary, Salary Cap & Minimum Team Salary) [of the CBA], if applicable." (Ibid., p. 7.)

3 National Football League, "NFL Owners Opt Out of CBA," news release, at http://www.nfl.com/news/story?id=09000d5d80868b78&template=without-video. In announcing that the owners voted to opt out of the current CBA, the NFL stated that "[t]he

current labor agreement does not adequately recognize the costs of generating the revenues of which the players receive the largest share; nor does the agreement recognize that those costs have increased substantially —and at an ever increasing rate—in recent years during a difficult economic climate in our country. As a result, under the terms of the current agreement, the clubs' incentive to invest in the game is threatened. There are substantial other elements of the deal that simply are not working. For example, as interpreted by the courts, the current CBA effectively prohibits the clubs from recouping bonuses paid to players who subsequently breach their player contracts or refuse to perform.... Our objective is to fix these problems in a new CBA...." (Ibid.) As reported by the *Pittsburgh Tribune-Review*, DeMaurice Smith, the head of the NFLPA, said that "'[t]he players of the National Football League are still in the dark about why this deal [collective bargaining agreement] isn't good enough.... And the easiest way to demonstrate any problem with the deal is the way any business in American demonstrates it: They turn over what the profit or loss numbers are. And if there's a problem with the model, we'll fix it." (Scott Brown and Carl Prine, "Union Chief: NFL Headed for Lockout," *Pittsburgh Tribune- Review*, August 19, 2009, at *http://www.pittsburghlive.com/x/ pittsburghtrib/sports/ steelers/s_638933.html.)*

[4] National Football League, "NFL Owners Opt Out of CBA."

[5]Associated Press, "NFLPA Advises Players About Potential '11 Lockout," *ESPN.com*, August 17, 2009, at http://sports.espn.go.com/espn/print?id=4404636&type=story.

[6] Averages were rounded.

[7] The 1982 strike was the first regular-season strike in the then 63-year history of the National Football League. Two previous "pre-season actions" occurred in 1970 and 1974 but did not extend beyond the start of the regular season.

[8] According to the Legislative Information System, neither resolution had a short title.

[9] Sen. Ted Stevens, "Professional Football Strike," remarks in the Senate, *Congressional Record*, vol. 128, part 17 (October 1, 1982), p. 26731.

[10] Ibid.

[11] Ibid., p. 26730.

[12] NFL Players Association, "A Strike vs. A Lockout," March 16, 2008, at http://nflplayers.com/user/content.aspx?fmid=178&lmid=443&pid=412&type=n&weigh=443,0,412,n.

[13] Sen. Robert Dole, "Senate Resolution (S.Res. 294)---Calling for An End to the 10-Day-Old Pro Football Strike," remarks in the Senate, *Congressional Record*, vol. 133, part 19 (October 1, 1987), p. 26146. According to the Legislative Information System, this resolution did not have a short title.

[14] Sen. Arlen Specter's rationale for S.Res. 291 was as follows: "In 1961, at the request of the NFL, Congress enacted the Sports Broadcasting Act (15 U.S.C. §§1291-95), which granted antitrust immunity to the NFL's pooling of revenues from sponsored television broadcasts. This permitted the NFL to enter into a series of leaguewide network television contracts.... At no time since the original grant of limited immunity 26 years ago, however, has the Department of Justice reviewed the NFL's telecasting practices to determine whether they are in compliance with the law. Since the law's enactment, there have been dramatic changes in the nature of telecommunications and in the NFL's telecasting practices.... Mr. President, I long have been concerned about the possibility that the NFL might remove a portion of its televised games from free broadcast television, available to the public at no charge, and offer them instead only to fans who can afford to pay—whether for cable service or on a 'pay-per-view' basis." (Sen. Arlen Specter, "Report on National Football League Telecasting," remarks in the Senate, *Congressional Record*, vol. 133, part 18 (September 29, 1987), p. 25637.)

[15] U.S. Congress, Senate Judiciary, Antitrust, Monopolies and Business Rights, *Antitrust Implications of the Recent NFL Television Contract*, hearing on S.Res. 291, 100th Cong., 1st sess., October 6, 1987, S.Hrg. 100-9 19 (Washington: GPO, 1988), p. 11. (Capitalization in original.)

[16] Arthur B. Modell was the president of the Cleveland Browns. He accompanied Mr. Rozelle.

[17] U.S. Congress, Senate Judiciary, Antitrust, Monopolies and Business Rights, *Antitrust Implications of the Recent NFL Television Contract*, p. 36. (Capitalization in original.)

[18] See "White House Efforts to Aid in Resolving the Strike" for additional information.

[19] Ted Keith, "Supreme Court Nominee Sonia Sotomayor Well Known in Sports," *SI.com*, May 26, 2009, at http://sportsillustrated.cnn.com/2009/baseball/mlb/05/26/sotomayor/index.html.

[20] Murray Chass, "Baseball Owners Quit Fight; Opening Day Is Set for April 26," *New York Times*, April 3, 1995, at http://www.lexis.com.

[21] Ibid.

[22] Sen. Howard Metzenbaum, "The Baseball Fans Protection Act of 1994," remarks in the Senate, *Congressional Record*, daily edition, August 11, 1994, p. S11342. Although S. 500 (103rd Congress), which was introduced in March 1993 and would have eliminated baseball's antitrust exemption, was not related to the baseball strike, it is mentioned here. Sen. Metzenbaum, upon introducing S. 500, related his perspective, as follows, regarding the exemption and labor relations: "8. How does the exemption affect relations with the players? Up until the mid-1970s, baseball needed the exemption in order to preserve the validity of the reserve clause. The reserve clause bound a player to the team which first signed him for the duration of his baseball career. In essence, the reserve clause was an agreement among the owners not to compete in the market for player services. Generally, such agreements would not pass muster under the antitrust laws. While a portion of major league players (those with more than 6 years experience) can become free agents, the bulk of big leaguers still have no opportunity to offer their services in a free market. Because these restrictions on the mobility of major leaguers are now included in the current collective bargaining agreement with the players, they would not be subject to challenge under the antitrust laws. However, the current labor agreement expires at the end of this year. If the owners and the players fail to reach an agreement, the owners could unilaterally impose restrictions on player mobility that would limit the competition for player services and thus probably run afoul of the antitrust laws. However, because of the exemption, the baseball players—unlike the football or basketball players— would have no ability to challenge the restrictions under the antitrust laws. Their only recourse against unreasonable restrictions on player mobility would be a strike. Thus, the antitrust exemption makes labor negotiations between the owners and the players more confrontational than they might be otherwise. That helps to explain why there has been a work stoppage (either a lockout or a strike) in baseball during every labor negotiation in the last five years.... Removing the exemption ... should foster more stable labor relations. As noted above, the antitrust exemption exacerbates the tendency of the owners and players to be confrontational in labor negotiations. A work stoppage is more likely in baseball than in the other sports because the players have no opportunity to bring an antitrust challenge against the restrictions on their mobility imposed by the owners. The owners have no reason to fear an antitrust suit, so their incentive to compromise is diminished; meanwhile, a strike is the players only option if the owners seek to unreasonably limit competition for player services." (Sen. Howard Metzenbaum, "Professional Baseball Antitrust Reform Act of 1993," remarks in the Senate, *Congressional Record*, daily edition, March 4, 1993, p. S2419.) Two additional bills introduced early in the 103rd Congress, H.R. 108 and H.R. 1549, also sought to apply antitrust laws to major league baseball and remove baseball from the Sports Broadcasting Act of 1961 (15 U.S.C. §§1291-1294), respectively. Since both bills were introduced several months before the commencement of the strike, and the bills' sponsors did not make statements about their measures, it is not known whether the status of labor negotiations were part of the rationale for either bill.

[23] Sen. Howard Metzenbaum, "The Baseball Fans Protection Act of 1994," p. S 11342.

[24] Ibid.

[25] Sen. Orrin Hatch, "The Baseball Fans Protection Act of 1994," remarks in the Senate, *Congressional Record*, daily edition, August 11, 1994, p. S11343.

[26] Ibid.

[27] Sen. Dennis DeConcini, "National Commission on Major League Baseball Act of 1994," remarks in the Senate, *Congressional Record*, daily edition, August 17, 1994, p. S 11994.

[28] Ibid.

[29] Ibid.

[30] Ibid.

[31] Rep. Mike Synar, "Introduction of the Baseball Fans and Communities Protection Act---Hon. Mike Synar," extension of remarks, *Congressional Record*, daily edition, August 18, 1994, p. E1764.

[32] U.S. Congress, House Committee on the Judiciary, *Baseball Fans and Communities Protection Act of 1994*, report to accompany H.R. 4994, 103rd Cong., 2nd sess., November 29, 1994, H.Rept. 103-871 (Washington: GPO, 1994), p. 34.

[33] Ibid., p. 2.

[34] Ibid., pp. 2-3.

[35] Ibid., p. 41.

[36] Ibid., p. 44.

[37] U.S. Congress, House Committee on Education and Labor, Subcommittee on Labor-Management Relations, *The Impact on Collective Bargaining of the Antitrust Exemption*, H.R. 5095, Major League Play Ball Act of 1995, 103rd Cong., 2nd sess., September 29, 1994, Serial No. 103-108 (Washington: GPO, 1995), p. 1.

[38] As demonstrated by the following statement, the subcommittee chairman believed that the parties to the dispute were not able to resolve the dispute themselves: "We have this strike that has more attention than steel strikes, rail strikes, coal strikes, and you are not sitting at the table and talking. It is extraordinarily unusual in American collective bargaining history. Folks just want to get you back to the table. If binding arbitration doesn't do it, okay, if breaking the antitrust thing doesn't do it, okay, you just want to be told to go back, okay, go back. Now. But you know what, that ain't going to get it, not with you guys, it ain't going to get it. You are too far apart. You can't come together."38 (Ibid., p. 113.)

[39] Rep. Pat Williams, "Play Baseball in 1995," extension of remarks, Congressional Record, daily edition, September 23, 1994, p. E1927.

[40] U.S. Congress, House Committee on Education and Labor, Subcommittee on Labor-Management Relations, The Impact on Collective Bargaining of the Antitrust Exemption, pp. 9-10.

[41] Ibid., p. 5.

[42] Ibid., p. 8.

[43] Ibid., pp. 3-4.

[44] Ibid., p. 117.

[45] Ibid., pp. 2-3, 115.

[46] Ibid., pp. 5-6.

[47] Ibid., p. 6.

[48] Ibid., p. 4.

[49] Ibid., p. 8.

[50] The subcommittee's initial hearing on baseball's antitrust exemption was held prior to the strike, on March 31, 1993.

[51] U.S. Congress, House Committee on the Judiciary, Subcommittee on Economic and Commercial Law, *Baseball's Antitrust Exemption (Part 2)*, 103rd Cong., 2nd sess., September 22, 1994, Serial No. 6 (Washington: GPO, 1994), p. 2.

[52] Ibid., p. 177.

[53] Ibid., pp. 153-154.

[54] Ibid., p. 2.

[55] Ibid., p. 25.

[56] Ibid., pp. 148-149. Witnesses included the executive director of the Major League Baseball Players Association, Donald M. Fehr, and the chairman of the Executive Council of Major

League Baseball, Allan H. "Bud" Selig. Hence, subcommittee members had an opportunity to address the parties to the dispute during the hearing.

[57] Ibid., p. 151.

[58] Ibid., p. 153.

[59] Rep. John Conyers, Jr., "Baseball Fans and Communities Protection Act of 1995," extension of remarks, *Congressional Record*, daily edition, January 5, 1995, p. E43.

[60] According to the Legislative Information System, this bill did not have a short title.

[61] Rep. Jim Bunning, "Major League Baseball," remarks in the House, *Congressional Record*, daily edition, January 17, 1995, p. H246.

[62] Rep. James A. Traficant, Jr., "Make Professional Baseball Subject to the Antitrust Laws," remarks in the House, *Congressional Record*, daily edition, January 5, 1995, p. E51.

[63] Rep. Pat Williams, "Play Ball," extension of remarks, *Congressional Record*, daily edition, January 5, 1995, pp. E49-E50.

[64] Rep. John J. LaFalce, "National Commission on Professional Baseball," remarks in the House, *Congressional Record*, daily edition, vol. 141, part 18 (January 30, 1995), p. E212.

[65] Ibid., p. E213.

[66] According to the Legislative Information System, this bill did not have a short title.

[67] Rep. Estaban Edward Torres, "Legislation to Repeal Anti-Trust Exemption Regarding Major League Baseball," extension of remarks, *Congressional Record*, daily edition, January 31, 1995, p. E236.

[68] Sen. Edward M. Kennedy, "Binding Arbitration to Settle Baseball Strike," remarks in the Senate, *Congressional Record*, daily edition, February 9, 1995, p. S2430.

[69] Sen. Daniel Patrick Moynihan, "National Pastime Preservation Act," remarks in the Senate, *Congressional Record*, daily edition, January 4, 1995, p. S 176. (Small capitals in original.)

[70] S. 415 and S. 416 are presented in a single subsection because one hearing was held for both bills.

[71] Sen. Strom Thurmond, "The Major League Baseball Antitrust Reform Act of 1995," remarks in the Senate, *Congressional Record*, daily edition, February 15, 1995, p. S2660.

[72] U.S. Congress, Senate Committee on the Judiciary, Subcommittee on Antitrust, Business Rights and Competition, *The Court-Imposed Major League Baseball Antitrust Exemption*, hearing on S. 415 and S. 416, 104th Cong., 1st sess., February 15, 1995, S. Hrg. 104-682 (Washington: GPO, 1996), p. 3.

[73] Ibid., pp. 2-3.

[74] Ibid., p. 1.

[75] Sen. Orrin Hatch, "The Professional Baseball Antitrust Reform Act of 1995," remarks in the Senate, *Congressional Record*, daily edition, February 14, 1995, p. S2659.

[76] Sen. Patrick Leahy, "The Major League Baseball Antitrust Reform Act of 1995," remarks in the Senate, *Congressional Record*, daily edition, February 15, 1995, p. S2661.

[77] Sen. Daniel Patrick Moynihan, "The Professional Baseball Antitrust Reform Act of 1995," remarks in the Senate, *Congressional Record*, daily edition, February 15, 1995, p. S2660.

[78] U.S. Congress, Senate Committee on the Judiciary, Subcommittee on Antitrust, Business Rights and Competition, *The Court-Imposed Major League Baseball Antitrust Exemption*, p. 7. (Italics in original.)

[79] Ibid., p. 73.

[80] Ibid., p. 68.

[81] Ibid., p. 6.

[82] Sen. Orrin Hatch, "Major League Baseball Antitrust Reform Act," remarks in the Senate, *Congressional Record*, daily edition, March 27, 1995, p. S4660; Sen. Strom Thurmond, "Major League Baseball Antitrust Reform Act," remarks in the Senate, *Congressional Record*, daily edition, March 27, 1995, p. S4660.

[83] U.S. Congress, Senate Committee on the Judiciary, *Major League Baseball Reform Act of 1995*, report to accompany S. 627, 104th Cong., 2nd sess., February 6, 1006, S.Rept. 104-231 (Washington:GPO, 1996), pp. 19-20.

[84] Ibid., pp. 2 1-22. (Italics in original.)

[85] Ibid., pp. 24-25.

[86] Ibid., p. 26.

[87] White House, "Press Briefing by Secretary of Labor Bob Reich, Bill Usery, Bud Selig, and Don Fehr," press release, October 14, 1994, http://clinton6.nara.gov/1994/10/1994-10-14-briefing-on-baseball-negotiations.html.

[88] U.S. President (Clinton), "Statement on the Baseball Strike," *Weekly Compilation of Presidential Documents*, vol. 31 (January 26, 1995), p. 124.

[89] David Hosansky, "President Swings and Misses at Baseball Strike," *Congressional Quarterly*, February 11, 1995, p. 449.

[90] U.S. President (Clinton), "Remarks on the Major League Baseball Strike and an Exchange with Reporters," *Weekly Compilation of Presidential Documents*, vol. 31 (February 7, 1995), p. 204.

[91] Ibid., p. 205.

[92] U.S. President (Clinton), "Message to the Congress Transmitting the 'Major League Baseball Restoration Act,'" *Weekly Compilation of Presidential Documents*, vol. 31 (February 9, 1995), p. 224.

[93] David Broughton, "NFL Labor Timeline," *Sports Business Journal*, September 1, 2008, p. 32.

[94] This section was written by Jon Shimabukuro, Legislative Attorney, American Law Division.

[95] 29 U.S.C. § 151 *et seq.*

[96] 29 U.S.C. § 158(d).

[97] *Id.*

[98] *See* The Developing Labor Law 1572 (John E. Higgins, Jr. et al. eds., 2006).

[99] 29 U.S.C. § 163.

[100] 29 U.S.C. § 173(b).

[101] *Id.*

[102] *See, e.g.,* Major League Play Ball Act, H.R. 5095, 103[d] Cong. (1994); Major League Baseball Restoration Act, H.R. 870, 104th Cong. (1995).

[103] For additional information on the Employee Free Choice Act, see CRS Report RS21887, *The Employee Free Choice Act*, by Jon O. Shimabukuro.

[104] *See, e.g.,* Jay J. Madrid & Jay G. Martin, Advantages of Using Mediation and Arbitration to Settle Environmental Disputes, *in* Environmental Dispute Resolution: An Anthology of Practical Solutions 46 (Ann L. MacNaughton & Jay G. Martin eds., 2002).

[105] *Id.*

[106] *See* Major League Play Ball Act, H.R. 5095, 103[d] Cong. (1994).

[107] This section was written by Janice E. Rubin, Legislative Attorney, American Law Division.

[108] 15 U.S.C. §§ 1291-1295 (P.L. 87-33 1).

[109] For more information on Major League Baseball's antitrust status, *see* CRS Report 98-820, *"Curt Flood Act of 1998 ": Application of Federal Antitrust Laws to Major League Baseball Players*, by Janice E. Rubin. Rubin. The Report also addresses the interaction between the two non-statutory exemptions/doctrines.

[110] The similar clause in NFL contracts is called the Rozelle Rule.

[111] The exemption does not apply to agreements between the leagues and cable or satellite media. Shaw v. Dallas Cowboys Football Club, Ltd., 1998 WL 419765 (E.D. Pa. 1998), *aff'd.*, 172 F.3d 299, 301 (3d Cir. 1999). According to the court of appeals, after it noted some of the act's legislative history, SBA's purpose was "to preserve the availability of [professional] games on *free* broadcast" (emphasis added).

[112] The section was amended in 1966 to permit the merger of the then-American Football League (AFL) and the NFL on the condition that the merger increase rather than decrease the number of professional football teams.

[113] U.S. Football League v. National Football League, 842 F.2d 1335, 1353 (2d Cir. 1988), *aff'g*, 644 F.Supp. 1040 (S.D.N.Y. 1986). Although multiple contracts *are* considered to be covered by § 1291, those which seek to limit the rights of individual teams to sell their

rights to games not included in a contract remain fully subject to the antitrust laws to the extent that they attempt to impose such limits (*e.g.*, Chicago Professional Sports Ltd. Partnership v. National Basketball Ass'n, 754 F.Supp. 1336, 1352 (N.D. Ill. 1991), *aff'd*, 961 F.2d 667 (7th Cir. 1992), *reh. denied; cert. denied*, 506 U.S. 954 (1992)).

[114] The prohibition is applicable to agreements with any station whose broadcast signal penetrates into the home territory, not only those actually located in the home territory. *See, e.g.*, WTWV, Inc. v. National Football League, 678 F.2d 142 (11th Cir. 1982).

The 1973 legislation (an amendment to the Communications Act) that required the leagues to lift the blackout of any pooled telecast if all the tickets available for purchase five days before the game were sold seventy-two hours prior to the game (47 U.S.C. § 331) was repealed in 1975, as mandated in the law, P.L. 93-107. The leagues have continued, however, to abide by that regime: "The sports leagues, wary about angering legions of sports fans who have become accustomed to watching sold-out home games on television, have, in effect, made the law permanent by voluntarily adhering to its terms for the past sixteen years. Few people, in fact, realize that the legislation expired at the end of the 1975 football season." (Dean A. Rosen, BACK TO THE FUTURE AGAIN: AN OBLIQUE LOOK AT THE SPORTS BROADCASTING ACT OF 1961, 13 (NO. 5) Entertainment L. Rep. 3, 6 (1991)).

[115] "The NFL is an unincorporated association of football teams ...." Stringer v. National Football League, 474 F.Supp.2d 894, 898 (S.D. Ohio 2007); *see also*, other cases in which the NFL is a party, including, *e.g.*, National Football League Players Ass'n v. National Football League Properties, Inc., 1991 WL 156280 (S.D.N.Y. 1991).

[116] Federal Baseball Club of Baltimore, Inc. v. National League of Professional Baseball Clubs, 259 U.S. 200, 208-209 (1922). The suit against the National League alleged it had acted in contravention of the antitrust laws to destroy the rival Federal League.

[117] In 1953, in Toolson v. New York Yankees, Inc. 346 U.S. 356, 357, the Court reaffirmed the position it had taken in Federal Baseball, although it did note that "if there are evils in this field which now warrant application to it of the antitrust laws it should be by legislation" and not by judicial action. By 1972, although the Court's "expanding interpretation of the commerce power" led it to state unequivocally that "professional baseball *is* a business ... engaged in interstate commerce," and despite the fact that in 1972 it considered the antitrust exempt status of professional baseball to be an "anomaly" and an "aberration," the "inconsistency or illogic" of the situation would have to be "remedied by the Congress and not by the Supreme Court" (Flood v. Kuhn, 407 U.S. 258, 282, 284, emphasis added; *see, also,* Piazza v. Major League Baseball, 831 F.Supp. 435 (E.D. Pa. 1993)).

[118] *See, e.g.*, Mackey v. National Football League, 543 F.2d 606 (8th Cir. 1976); Smith v. Pro-Football, Inc., 593 F.2d 1173 (1978); Connell Construction Co. v. Plumbers & Steamfitters Union, 421 U.S. 616 (1975).

[119] 421 U.S. 616, 622 (1975).

[120] *Mackey, supra,* note 12, 543 F.2d at 6 16-17.

[121] *Id.* at 611.

[122] Flood v. Kuhn, 316 F.Supp. 271, 275-76 (S.D.N.Y.1970).

[123] Flood v. Kuhn, 407 U.S. 258 (1972).

[124] "The Court has expressed concern [over the years, in several prior opinions] about the confusion and the retroactivity problems that inevitably would result with a judicial overturning of Federal Baseball [Club of Baltimore, Inc. v. National League of Professional Baseball Clubs, 259 U.S. 200 (1922)]. It has voiced a preference that if any change is to be made, it come by legislative action that, by its nature, is only prospective in operation. ... The Court [has] noted ... that the slate with respect to baseball is not clean. Indeed, it has not been clean for half a century. ... This emphasis and this concern are still with us. We continue to be loath, 50 years after Federal Baseball and almost two decades after Toolson [v. New York Yankees, Inc. 346 U.S. 356 (1953)], to overturn those cases judicially when Congress, by its positive inaction, has allowed those decisions to stand for so long and, far

beyond mere inference and implication, has clearly evinced a desire not to disapprove them legislatively. Accordingly, we adhere once again to Federal Baseball and Toolson and to their application to professional baseball. ... *If there is any inconsistency or illogic in all this, it is an inconsistency and illogic of long standing that is to be remedied by the Congress and not by this Court.*" 407 U.S. at 283-284 (emphasis added).

[125] P.L. 105-297, codified at 15 U.S.C. § 26b. Its predecessor history includes, for example, the Final Report of the House Select Committee on Professional Sports (94th Congress), which had concluded that "adequate justification does not exist for baseball's special exemption from the antitrust laws ... [and] the exemption should be removed in the context of overall sports antitrust reform" (*Inquiry into Professional Sports* (January3, 1977) at 60). Among the first responses to that conclusion was H.R. 2129, prompted, according to its sponsor, by both the Court's and the Committee Report's "invitations" to Congress; H.R. 2129 would have legislatively "repealed" the entirety of baseball's antitrust exemption (*i.e.*, made the antitrust laws applicable to professional baseball), not merely the exemption as it has been applied to the "reserve" clause. *See* 125 CONG. REC. 2521 (February 13, 1979).

In the 103d Congress, several bills to end or limit the exemption either remained pending in House and Senate Committees or were reported but not acted upon by either the full House or Senate. For a more detailed listing of the bills, *see* CRS Report 98-820, *"Curt Flood Act of 1998": Application of Federal Antitrust Laws to Major League Baseball Players*, by Janice E. Rubin.

In the 104th Congress, which was energized by the 1994 strike, more than a dozen measures to either make the antitrust laws unqualifiedly and generally applicable to professional baseball, or applicable only to specific issues (*e.g.*, player- management relations), were introduced but not acted upon.

[126] But explicitly *not* to minor league players pursuant to 15 U.S.C. §§ 26b(b) and 26b(b)(1), which state that "No court shall rely on the enactment of this section as a basis for changing the application of the antitrust laws ... any conduct, acts, practices, or agreements [concerning] the business of organized professional baseball relating to or affecting employment to play baseball at the minor league level," and specifically not to "any reserve clause as applied to minor league players."

[127] 15 U.S.C. § 26b(a).

In: Professional and Collegiate Sports
Editor: Thomas M. Miller ISBN: 978-1-61122-191-6

Chapter 2

NFL, MEMBER TEAMS NOT A "SINGLE ENTITY" IMMUNE TO PROSECUTION UNDER SECTION 1 OF THE SHERMAN ACT: *AMERICAN NEEDLE, INC. V. NATIONAL FOOTBALL LEAGUE*

Janice E. Rubin

SUMMARY

In a decision that had the potential to upset decades of antitrust law, and also to have a broad impact beyond the immediate consequences for the litigating parties, the Supreme Court ruled, on May 24, 2010, that the intellectual-property licensing activities of the National Football League (NFL or League) and its member teams must be treated as those of separate entities whose cooperation and joint decisions are amenable to antitrust prosecution under Section 1 of the Sherman Act, which prohibits contracts or conspiracies "in restraint of trade" (*American Needle, Inc. v. National Football League,* 560 U.S. ___ (2010)). There had been some concern that a contrary ruling—a finding that the NFL's member teams are but "divisions" of an unincorporated NFL and so are incapable of ever conspiring with either each other or the League itself—could have affected existing antitrust jurisprudence concerning the status of entities in sports leagues generally, and also of those entities involved in cooperative or joint venture activity in such diverse areas as real estate services, financial services, and health care.

The immediate issues in the case were the teams' creation in 1963 of NFL Properties (NFLP) to license and market their team-owned intellectual property (primarily team logos); and their subsequent authorization for NFLP to replace the multiple, non-exclusive contracts it had awarded for the manufacture of team-logoed headwear with a single, exclusive contract. American Needle, a holder of one of the former, non-exclusive contracts sued, alleging violation of Section 1. Both parties relied on interpretations of the 1984 decision in *Copperweld Corp. v. Independence Tube Corp.* (467 U.S. 752) to support their arguments. The League successfully argued in both the U.S. District Court for Northern Illinois and the U.S. Court of Appeals for the Seventh Circuit that its structure should be considered analogous to the one analyzed in *Copperweld*; that case held that a parent corporation is incapable of conspiring, in violation of the antitrust laws, with its corporate division(s), or the divisions with each other, because all of those entities share a unity of economic interest. NFL teams, the League insisted, should be similarly viewed—as merely "divisions" of the unincorporated-parent NFL. American Needle had stressed the teams' status as "independently owned and controlled for-profit businesses that do compete, and are capable of competing with each other in numerous ways." The lower federal courts ruled in favor of the NFL because they believed that since team cooperation to produce the NFL product (football games) is indispensable, the teams, even though separately owned business corporations, are the practical equivalents of *Copperweld's* divisions of a corporate parent.

A unanimous *American Needle* Supreme Court disagreed with the NFL, reversing the lower-court decisions and remanding the case for trial. The Court was persuaded that the League's 32 teams, contrary to the NFL's characterization, are separately owned businesses that are engaged in competition for, for example, players, fans, and gate receipts; it quoted *Copperweld* to emphasize that because the teams are "separate economic actors pursuing separate economic interests," they cannot possess the unity of economic interest that would save them from Section 1 scrutiny: the antitrust legality of their cooperative activity must be judged under Section 1 of the Sherman Act, rather than under Section 2, which addresses the unilateral conduct of monopolists. At the same time, the Court specifically recognized that the teams' necessary and "perfectly sensibly justified" cooperation, for example, in the "production and scheduling of games," would provide the basis for rule of reason versus *per se* analysis of those or other cooperative agreements alleged to violate Section 1 of the Sherman Act. Moreover, the opinion observed, the League's activities are not necessarily doomed to violation-of-Section-1-status because "joint ventures and other cooperative agreements are ... not usually unlawful ... where the agreement ... is necessary to market the product at all."

BACKGROUND AND INTRODUCTION

The teams of the National Football League (NFL or League) formed NFL Properties (NFLP) in 1963 to aid in the promotion of the NFL brand, including the manufacture, licensing, and marketing of team- and league-logoed, trademarked clothing and merchandise. Originally, the licenses granted by NFLP were non-exclusive (i.e., granted simultaneously to several parties); American Needle, a headwear manufacturer, was one of the non-exclusive licensees for several years. In 2000, the teams authorized NFLP to solicit bids for, and then grant, a single, exclusive license for the manufacture of headwear; when the license was awarded to Reebok, American Needle, one of the non-renewed, non-exclusive licensees, sued the NFL, NFLP, the individual teams, and Reebok, alleging, in pertinent part, that the teams' actions in creating NFLP violated Section 1 of the Sherman Act.[1] The NFL/team response was the assertion that as subsidiary members of an unincorporated association, the teams were legally incapable of conspiring either with each other or with the League.

American Needle was rebuffed in both the U.S District Court for Northern Illinois[2] and in the U.S. Court of Appeals for the Seventh Circuit.[3] Although the NFL was successful in those courts, it did not oppose American Needle's petition for *certiorari* in the Supreme Court.

The case had been carefully watched, given that a Supreme Court ruling endorsing the NFL's "single entity" argument would likely have had an impact on the application of the antitrust laws not only to other (professional) sports leagues and their decisions concerning, for example, player services, ticket pricing, stadium parking fees, and merchandise sales; but also to any business entity—especially those in such areas as financial services, real estate services, or health care— participating or contemplating participation in joint activities.[4]

Relevant Antitrust Statutes

Sections 1 and 2 of the Sherman Act[5] address, respectively, cooperative activity and unilateral activity by monopolists or would-be monopolists. Although Section 1 prohibits, without exception, contracts or conspiracies "in restraint of trade," the courts have created two classes of antitrust analysis—*per se* and rule of reason. Those "agreements or practices which because of their pernicious effect on competition and lack of any redeeming virtue are conclusively presumed to be unreasonable and therefore illegal under Sherman Act without elaborate inquiry as to precise harm they have caused or business excuse for their use."[6]

They are analyzed as *per se* (automatic) violations for which there can be no justification. In other words, if "[a]practice facially appears to be one that would always or almost always tend to restrict competition and decrease output [rather than one that would] 'increase economic efficiency and render markets more, rather than less, competitive,'"[7] it will be deemed a *per se* offense. *Per se* offenses (there are not many) include price fixing, market allocation, and boycotts or joint refusals to deal; generally, only *per se* antitrust offenses are prosecuted criminally.

On the other hand, courts have long recognized that

> the legality of an agreement or regulation cannot be determined by so simple a test, as whether it restrains competition. Every agreement concerning trade, every regulation of trade, restrains. To bind, to restrain, is of their very essence. The true test of legality is whether the restraint imposed is such as merely regulates and perhaps thereby promotes competition or whether it is such as may suppress or even destroy competition. To determine that question the court must ordinarily consider the facts peculiar to the business to which the restraint is applied; its condition before and after the restraint was imposed; the nature of the restraint and its effect, actual or probable.[8]

Such agreements are analyzed as rule of reason offenses, and usually receive much more extensive scrutiny than do the relatively quickly disposed of *per se* offenses. Pursuant to rule of reason analysis, if, on balance, the precompetitive effects of the activity outweigh the anticompetitive results, the activity is found to be "reasonable," and even if it effectively violates the antitrust laws, it is deemed not unlawful.

Section 2 prohibits "monopolization" or "attempted monopolization,"[9] either of which may be engaged in by a single entity, and neither of which requires, but *may* involve, an agreement between two or more parties. As the Court has noted, with respect to the purpose and use of Section 2, "[t]he conduct of a single firm is governed by § 2 alone and is unlawful *only* when it threatens actual monopolization. It is not enough that a single firm appears to "restrain trade" unreasonably, for even a vigorous competitor may leave that impression."[10]

There are no *per se* offenses associated with Section 2.

Not surprisingly, therefore, an entity with multiple members would prefer to be considered as a single entity amenable to prosecution only under Section 2 of the Sherman Act (the position, in fact, advanced by defendant/respondent NFL), rather than as multiple, separate entities that are legally capable of unlawful cooperation or agreement, and so always amenable to civil suit and/or criminal prosecution under Section 1 (plaintiff/appellant American Needle's argument).

Copperweld Corp. v. Independence Tube Corp.

Throughout the *American Needle* case both parties relied on interpretations of the language and holding in *Copperweld Corp. v. Independence Tube Corp.*[11] to support their arguments.

Copperweld addressed a situation in which a corporation (Copperweld) was alleged to have unlawfully conspired, in violation of Section 1 of the Sherman Act, with a division it created to house its acquisition of another corporation (Regal Tube). Refusing to find a violation, the Supreme Court explained:

> The distinction between unilateral and concerted conduct is necessary for a proper understanding of the terms "contract, combination ... or conspiracy" in § 1. Nothing in the literal meaning of those terms excludes coordinated conduct among officers or employees of the same company. But it is perfectly plain that an internal "agreement" to implement a single, unitary firm's policies does not raise the antitrust dangers that § 1 was designed to police. *The officers of a single firm are not separate economic actors pursuing separate economic interests, so agreements among them do not suddenly bring together economic power that was previously pursuing divergent goals.* Coordination within a firm is as likely to result from an effort to compete as from an effort to stifle competition. In the marketplace, such coordination may be necessary if a business enterprise is to compete effectively. For these reasons, officers or employees of the same firm do not provide the plurality of actors imperative for a § 1 conspiracy.[12]

Previously in its opinion, the Court had noted the rationale for treating concerted behavior "more strictly" than unilateral behavior: *"It deprives the marketplace of the independent centers of decisionmaking that competition assumes and demands."* [13]

Although the situation in Copperweld involved a corporate division, the Court also discussed the status of a corporation and its wholly owned subsidiar(ies), a scenario that the NFL sought to convince the *American Needle* Court was analogous to its own. The *Copperweld* Court had noted that any court reviewing the antitrust legality of a conspiracy alleged to be in violation of Section 1 must not be overly concerned with the form of corporate structure but must look to its substance: "The economic, legal, or other considerations that lead corporate management to choose one structure over the other [unincorporated division or wholly owned subsidiary] are not relevant to whether the enterprise's conduct seriously threatens competition."[14]

Both "the ultimate interests of ...[either an unincorporated division and those of a wholly owned subsidiary] ... and the parent are identical,"[15] as is the parent's ability to exercise complete control over either.

AMERICAN NEEDLE IN THE LOWER FEDERAL COURTS[16]

The District Court

The United States District Court for Northern Illinois seemed to make much of the fact that plaintiff American Needle "did not claim that the NFL and its 32 teams [had] ... acted improperly" in the initial creation of NFLP and the delegation to it of "the authority to grant licenses" for the teams' intellectual property; allegations of conspiracy in restraint of trade in violation of Section 1 were confined to the decision by NFL Properties to grant an exclusive license. That distinction was quickly rejected by the court: "The issue ... is whether the 32 teams can agree on designating a common actor to exploit their various intellectual property rights."[17]

Granting the League and the teams' motion to dismiss, the district court issued both a conclusion directed specifically to that facet of the teams' actions: "the facts ... lead undeniably to the conclusion that the NFL and the teams act as a single entity *in licensing their intellectual property,"*[18] as well as earlier, more broadly directed statements. For example, "*Copperweld* casts considerable doubt upon prior lower court decisions broadly rejecting the single entity concept."[19]

But the district court also appeared to rely on *Copperweld* only to support the assertion that "[d]elegated decision-making does not deprive the marketplace of independent centers of decision-making."[20]

The second district court decision was limited to disposing, favorably to the NFL, of the remaining counts of the complaint, which alleged monopolization in violation of Section 2.

The Court of Appeals

Affirming the district court dismissal, the U.S. Court of Appeals for the Seventh Circuit characterized American Needle's assertion that "the NFL teams can be a single entity only if the teams have 'a complete unity of interest'" as a "legal proposition that we have rejected as 'silly.'"[21] While it is true that "the Supreme Court in *Copperweld* was concerned about the anti-competitive effects that collective action might introduce into the market," it is just as true that the foundation of that concern was "whether the conduct in question deprives the marketplace of the independent sources of economic control that competition assumes."[22] Having already noted that there might well be "competing interests" among the entities involved, even among bona fide divisions of the same company, the court of appeals was not persuaded that the ability of the NFL teams to compete with regard to the merchandising of their intellectual property (logos et al.) should automatically foreclose the option of considering them as a single entity for purposes of the proper use of the antitrust laws: "the NFL teams can function only as one source of economic power when collectively producing NFL football."[23]

The court also relied on arguments set out in Supreme Court opinions[24] to the effect that the NFL as an entity competes with other league sports, to buttress its finding that the NFL cannot produce the several sources of independent economic control that would necessitate the use of Section 1.

Finally, the court disposed of American Needle's argument that even if the NFL and its member teams were considered as a single entity subject to Section 2's prohibition against monopolization, their joint action in authorizing an exclusive headwear licensing contract constituted conduct prohibited by that section: "an antitrust claim based on a single firm's denial of a license to a trademark would readily be dismissed ...."[25]

AMERICAN NEEDLE V. NFL IN THE SUPREME COURT

A unanimous Supreme Court, per Justice Stevens, defined the issue:

> As the case comes to us, we have only a narrow issue to decide: whether the NFL respondents are capable of engaging in a "contract, combination ... or conspiracy" as defined by § 1 of the Sherman Act ..., or, as we have sometimes phrased it, whether the alleged activity by the NFL respondents "must be viewed as that of a single enterprise for purposes of § 1." *Copperweld* ..., 467 U.S. 752, 771 ....[26]

The ruling answered "yes" to the first "whether" and "no" to the second, deciding against the successful-in-the-lower-federal-courts NFL and in favor of the position taken by American Needle.

Summarizing the cases—ending with *Copperweld*—in which the Court had addressed the "now- efunct doctrine known as the 'intraenterprise conspiracy doctrine,'"[27] Justice Stevens noted that the Court had previously concluded that the doctrine "was inconsistent with the 'basic distinction between concerted and independent action.'"[28] But he also noted that the Court has always looked at the functional (as opposed to the formal, legal) relationships among the entities litigating before it in order to determine whether competition had been, unlawfully, adversely affected:

> We have long held that concerted action under § 1 does not turn simply on whether the parties involved are legally distinct entities. Instead, we have eschewed such formalistic distinctions in favor of a functional consideration of how the parties involved in the alleged anticompetitive conduct *actually operate*.
>
> As a result, we have repeatedly found instances in which members of a legally single entity violated § 1 when the entity was controlled by a group of competitors and served, in essence, as a vehicle for ongoing concerted activity.[29]

Accordingly, the opinion proceeded to look at the "competitive reality"[30] existing in the NFL and its member teams, and to the purpose of Section 1 to determine whether their concerted actions are of the kind that the provision was enacted to deter and punish. The teams, albeit related by virtue of their status in the NFL, "compete with one another, not only on the playing field, but to attract fans, for gate receipts and for contracts with managerial and playing personnel."[31]

Especially relevant to the case before the Court, the teams can and do compete in the market for intellectual property (team-logoed or otherwise trademarked merchandise, etc.): "[t]o a firm making hats, the Saints and the Colts are two potentially competing suppliers of valuable trademarks. In the words of *Copperweld*, therefore, "'their general corporate actions are guided or determined by 'separate corporate consciousness,' and 'their objectives are' not 'common.'"[32]

The Court was not unmindful of the fact that there may be a common interest in the joint licensing of team/NFL trademarks, or in other cooperative action:

> Other features of the NFL may also save agreements amongst the teams. We have recognized, for example, "that the interest in maintaining a competitive balance" among "athletic teams is legitimate and important," *NCAA* [v. *Board of Regents*], 468 U.S. 85,117 .... While that same interest applies to the teams in the NFL, it does not justify treating them as a single entity for § 1 purposes when it comes to the marketing of the teams' individually owned intellectual property. It is, however, unquestionably an interest that may well justify a variety of collective decisions made by the teams.[33]

Nevertheless, Justice Stevens was constrained to point out that "illegal restraints often are in the common interests of the parties to the restraint," and that "[t]he justification for cooperation is not relevant to whether that cooperation is concerted or independent action."[34]

Having thus made clear that substance versus form will determine whether collective action is the kind of concerted action appropriately analyzed under Section 1 of the Sherman Act, and that the NFL/team intellectual-property licensing activities would continue to be analyzed under that section, Justice Stevens sought to reassure the NFL that "[f]ootball teams that need to cooperate are not trapped by antitrust law." He emphasized the Court's view that "collective decisions" by the League and its teams are "perfectly sensible" given the "special characteristics" of the football industry.[35] Therefore, although the antitrust analysis will generally occur under Section 1, the appropriate mode of analysis will almost certainly be the "flexible" rule of reason rather than the more rigid *per se* analysis.

The need to examine the League/team collective action in licensing their respective and common trademarks under Section 1 led the Court to remand the case to the U.S. Court of Appeals for the Seventh Circuit, which will, in turn, likely remand to the U.S. District Court for Northern Illinois for trial.

End Notes

[1] 15 U.S.C. § 1.

[2] American Needle, Inc. v. New Orleans Louisiana Saints. 496 F. Supp.2d 941 (N.D Ill. 2007); 533 F. Supp.2d 7901 (N.D. Ill. 2007) (both granting defendants' motions to dismiss).

[3] 538 F.3d 736 (7th Cir. 2008).

[4] *E.g.*: "The outcome of this case is of great interest to the [NFL] Players' Association. The antitrust settlement in the NFL is about to expire in 2011. The labor agreements in MLB [Major League Baseball], the NBA [National Basketball Association], and the NHL [National Hockey League] are similarly set to expire in or around 2011. The NFL owners' appeal in this case is a Trojan horse designed to free sports team owners from Section 1 scrutiny so they can restrain competition with impunity in the market for player services. If the broad single entity defense advanced by the owners were adopted, decades of antitrust precedents that have protected competition for player services would be reversed, the benefits that both players and consumers have gained from competitive markets would be jeopardized, and labor disputes and work stoppages would likely ensue." Brief Amici Curiae for the Players' Associations of the NFL, MLB, NBA, and the NHL in Support of Petitioner American Needle at 2; and, "[i]f the Court affirms, and particularly if it does so in explicit reliance on [Texaco v.] Dagher (547 U.S. 1 (2006) [a case in which the Court found no price fixing on the part of Texaco and Shell, when the joint venture they had formed to market gasoline sold their separate brands to stations at identical prices], *then American Needle could, as a practical matter, do significant damage to the enforceability of Section 1 of the Sherman Act; it could in effect immunize significant swaths of concerted conduct among competitors.* It would imply that comparatively unintegrated arrangements, like trademark licensing agreements among the NFL member teams, are just as 'economically integrated' as the defendants' joint venture in Dagher. In short order we would see horizontal arrangements throughout the economy purporting to have 'integrated' around some shared common purpose." Chris Sagers, *American Needle, Dagher, and the Evolving Antitrust Theory of The Firm: What Will Become of Section 1?* ANTITRUST SOURCE , Aug. 2009 (emphasis added) http://new.abanet.org/antitrust/Searchable%20Antitrust%20Library/antitrust-source-Aug09-Sagers8-12f.pdf. The announcement of a June 29, 2010 American Bar Association Teleconference titled, "*American Needle v. NFL*: Impact on Joint Ventures," refers to "a highly anticipated decision" which "may impact joint ventures under a § 1 Sherman Act analysis."

[5] 15 U.S.C. §§ 1 and 2.

[6] Northern Pac. Ry. Co. v. U.S. 356 U.S. 1, 78 (1958).

[7] Broadcast Music, Inc. v. Columbia Broadcasting System, Inc. 441 U.S. 1, 19-20 (1979), *quoting and citing,* United States v. United States Gypsum Co., 438 U.S. 422, 441, n. 16 (1978).

[8] Board of Trade of City of Chicago v. U.S. 246 U.S. 231, 238 (1918).

[9] The statute does *not* prohibit monopoly, or the fact of being a monopolist, only conduct that may be characterized as "guilty behavior" designed to unlawfully achieve, maintain (*e.g.*, via predatory pricing behavior), or extend a monopoly, even a lawful one.

[10] Copperweld Corp. v. Independence Tube Corp., 467 U.S. 752, 767 (1984) (note omitted, emphasis added).

[11] 467 U.S. 752 (1984).

[12] 467 U.S. at 769 (emphasis added).

[13] 467 U.S. at 769 (emphasis added).

[14] *Id.* at 772.

[15] *Id.*

[16] *Cf,* notes 2 and 3, *supra.*

[17] 496 F. Supp. 2d at 942-943.

[18] *Id.* at 944 (emphasis added).

[19] *Id.* at 943.

[20] *Id.* at 943. Moreover, the court also noted, pointedly, that "American Needle, Inc. does not suggest that it ever dealt with any of the teams as independent organizations" (*Id.* at 944).

[21] 538 F.3d 736, 743. The reference is to the Seventh Circuit interpretation of *Copperweld* in Chicago Professional Sports Ltd. Partnership v. National Basketball Ass'n 95 F.3d 593 (7th Cir. 1996): "Although that phrase ['complete unity of interest'] appears in *Copperweld*, the Court offered it as a statement of fact about the parent-subsidiary relation, not as a proposition of law about the limits of permissible cooperation. As a proposition of law, it would be silly. Even a single firm contains many competing interests."

[22] 538 F.3d at 743.

[23] *Id.*

[24] Most notably, National Collegiate Athletic Ass'n v. Bd. of Regents (468 U.S. 85, 101 (1984)), which quoted Robert Bork in THE ANTITRUST PARADOX (1978); and the dissenting opinion of Justice Rehnquist in Nat'l Football League v. No. American Soccer League (459 U.S. 1074, 1077 (1982)).

[25] 538 F.3d at 744, *quoting* from Gregory J. Werden, "Antitrust Analysis of Joint Ventures: An Overview," 66 ANTITRUST L.J. 701, 730-31 (1998).

[26] American Needle v. National Football League, 560 U.S. ___, ___ (2010), slip opinion at 4, 2010 WL 2025207 at *5.

[27] Slip opinion at 7, 2010 WL2025207 at *6.

[28] Slip opinion at 9, 2010 WL 2025207 at *7, *quoting* from *Copperweld*, 467 U.S. at 767.

[29] Slip opinion at 6, 2010 WL 2025207 at *6 (emphasis added).

[30] Slip opinion at 11, 2010 WL 2025207 at *9

[31] Slip opinion at 12, 2010 WL 2025207 at *9.

[32] *Id.*, *quoting* from 467 U.S. at 771.

[33] Slip opinion at 19, 2010 WL 2025207 at *13.

[34] Slip opinion at 13, 14, 2010 WL 2025207 at *10, *11.

[35] Slip opinion at 18, 2010 WL 2025207 at *12, *citing* and *quoting* the "special characteristics" language of his own dissent in Brown v. Pro Football, Inc., 518 U.S. 231, 252 (1996), a case in which the Court found that the nonstatutory labor exemption from antitrust liability permitted the League to impose certain salary conditions on substitute players after collective bargaining on the issue between the League and the Players' Association had not produced any results.

In: Professional and Collegiate Sports
Editor: Thomas M. Miller
ISBN: 978-1-61122-191-6

Chapter 3

TAX PREFERENCES FOR COLLEGIATE SPORTS

Congressional Budget Office

SUMMARY

Colleges and universities generally qualify for preferential treatment under the federal income tax. The income of nonprofit private and public postsecondary schools is exempt from taxation, and gifts to those schools are generally tax-deductible to the donor. Those tax preferences stem from the schools' educational mission. But concerns have arisen that some activities undertaken by colleges and universities are only loosely connected to educating students and might be viewed as unrelated to the schools' tax-favored purpose.

One such activity is intercollegiate sports. Long viewed as an integral component of higher education, sports in many universities have become highly commercialized. Successful athletic programs are very rewarding financially: The National Collegiate Athletic Association (NCAA) men's basketball tournament alone garnered about $143 million in revenue for athletic departments in 2008, and college football bowl games generated a similar amount.

Such large sums raise the questions of whether those sports programs have become side businesses for schools and, if they have, whether the same tax preferences should apply to them as to schools in general. This Congressional Budget Office (CBO) paper compares athletic departments' share of revenue from commercial sources with that of the rest of the schools' activities to assess the degree of their commercialization. It also discusses some of the issues that might arise if the Congress decided to alter the treatment of intercollegiate sports programs in the tax code.

This analysis focuses on the athletic programs of colleges and universities in the NCAA's Division I—those that have the largest sports programs and, consequently, are most likely to engage in commercial activities. Broadly defined, commercial activities provide a good or service in exchange for a fee in a market that also includes taxed businesses; in sports, those activities include ticket sales, shared revenue from championship games, sales of media rights, and advertising. In conducting this study, CBO relied on two sources of data on the revenue generated by the athletic programs of Division I schools: budget reports from the athletic departments of NCAA schools collected in 2006 by the *Indianapolis Star* newspaper under the Freedom of Information Act and data on total revenue for those schools from the Department of Education.

The study also examines the issues that might arise if policymakers decided that some or all of the activities of the schools' athletic programs were primarily commercial rather than educational—a decision that would greatly reduce or eliminate the rationale for giving those activities preferential tax treatment. The Congress could change the tax treatment of revenue from those activities in several ways, for example, by limiting the deduction for contributions, limiting the use of tax-exempt bonds, or limiting the exemption from income taxation.

On the basis of its analysis, CBO concludes the following:

- Athletic departments in NCAA Division I schools derive a considerably larger share of their revenue from commercial activities than do other parts of the universities.
- In the case of Division IA schools (a subset of schools in Division I that meet NCAA requirements for football programs), 60 percent to 80 percent of athletic departments' revenue comes from activities that can be described as commercial. That proportion is seven to eight times that for the rest of the schools' activities and programs, suggesting that their sports programs may have crossed the line from educational to commercial endeavors. Revenue from commercial

activities accounts for a much smaller share of athletic department revenue (20 percent to 30 percent) for schools in the rest of Division I.

- Nonetheless, removing the major tax preferences currently available to university athletic departments would be unlikely to significantly alter the nature of those programs or garner much tax revenue even if the sports programs were classified, for tax purposes, as engaging in unrelated commercial activity. As long as athletic departments remained a part of the larger nonprofit or public university, schools would have considerable opportunity to shift revenue, costs, or both between their taxed and untaxed sectors, rendering efforts to tax that unrelated income largely ineffective. Changing the tax treatment of income from certain sources, such as corporate sponsorships or royalties from sales of branded merchandise, would be more likely to affect only the most commercial teams; it would also create less opportunity for shifting revenue or costs.

CURRENT TAX TREATMENT OF THE ACTIVITIES OF COLLEGES AND UNIVERSITIES

As nonprofit institutions, colleges and universities are granted a variety of federal tax preferences that are designed to support their educational purpose, which has social as well as private benefits. Those preferences are not unlimited. The law has consistently attempted to balance the advantages of preferential federal tax treatment for nonprofit organizations against the possibility that those preferences could be used to engage in commercial activities that compete with taxable businesses.

Institutions of higher education, both public and private, benefit from several types of preferential tax treatment. Nonprofit private schools, like other nonprofits defined in section 501(c)(3) of the Internal Revenue Code, are exempt from the federal income tax, are eligible to receive charitable contributions that the donor may deduct, and may use tax-exempt debt to finance capital expenditures. Public colleges and universities receive broadly similar tax preferences; as state or local government entities, they are exempt from federal income taxation, are eligible for deductible contributions, and may have access to tax-exempt debt.

Like other nonprofit organizations, colleges and universities receive those preferences because they serve a public purpose. For institutions of higher learning, that public purpose is clearly education, which has traditionally included education through participation in athletics. Education is associated with a wide range of favorable outcomes. Investment in human capital through education confers a considerable private benefit on the individual, in the form of higher income and better health.[1] Education also creates public benefits for the community as a whole, including a more skilled workforce, increased economic growth, and greater social mobility.[2] An individual's decision regarding how much education to invest in will depend on his or her private benefit alone; in the absence of government intervention, that decision will yield fewer public benefits than is socially desirable. The favorable tax treatment of educational institutions, including those providing postsecondary education, is one way in which policymakers may be able to offset some of the potential underinvestment in human capital and subsidize the social benefits of education.

Because providing such benefits is the primary justification for nonprofit institutions' federal tax preferences, the government has a clear interest in ensuring that those preferences are used to facilitate activities that yield those benefits and not other activities. Thus, the federal income tax exemption for nonprofits is limited to income earned from the pursuit of the purpose that renders them eligible for the exemption, referred to as related income. Income earned from activities that are not substantially related to the performance of the exempt purpose is not tax-exempt and is subject to the corporate income tax on unrelated business income, commonly referred to as the unrelated business income tax (UBIT). That tax was enacted in 1950, at least partially in response to New York University's acquisition of Mueller's, the noodle and pasta company. The purchase of that previously taxable business contributed to the perception that nonprofit-owned businesses, facing lower costs because of their tax-exempt status and other federal subsidies, would be able to underprice taxable businesses, leading to unfair competition and the erosion of the corporate tax base.[3]

Policymakers at that time were also concerned that allowing charitable institutions to pursue commercial activities on a tax-exempt basis would encourage them to allocate an excessive amount of resources to those activities rather than to their charitable purpose. To that end, the law they enacted subjected income from commercial enterprises to the UBIT even if that income was used to finance the primary mission of an exempt organization. For colleges and universities, for example, the income they earn from tuition, research grants, passive investment income (which includes royalties, interest, and capital gains), contributions, and athletics is considered related to the exempt purpose and is therefore tax-exempt, but income earned from operating a restaurant that serves the general public is not, even if the profits are used to provide educational services for students.

Because public universities operate under the auspices of state governments, laws regarding state commercial enterprises may also be relevant to the commercialization of their activities. In general, the Internal Revenue Service (IRS) has never considered state commercial enterprises of any type taxable, even if they are separately incorporated, because their operation is invariably classified as an essential state function and the income accrues to the state government. The Internal Revenue Code, however, specifically makes state colleges and universities subject to the UBIT. That situation creates an anomaly: Any other state entity running a trade or business would not be subject to the UBIT and taxation, but a state college running the same unrelated business would be subject to the tax under current law.

Like the exemption from federal income taxation, the deductibility of charitable contributions to a nonprofit entity is subject to some limits when the contribution resembles a commercial transaction. In general, contributions given to a nonprofit in exchange for a good or service are nondeductible for the donor. Some donations to athletic departments are made to obtain the right to buy game tickets or preferential seating, and in 1986 the IRS ruled that such contributions were in return for a "sub-stantial benefit" and were therefore nondeductible. In 1988, however, the Congress enacted legislation that explicitly permitted donors to deduct 80 percent of those contributions under section 170 of the Internal Revenue Code.

COMPARING COMMERCIALIZATION IN ATHLETIC DEPARTMENTS AND OTHER UNIVERSITY ACTIVITIES

This paper does not consider the possible commercial nature of a college or university as a whole.[4] Rather, the analysis takes the primarily noncommercial nature of the entire institution as a given and focuses on the activities of athletic programs. Specifically, this analysis addresses the concern that athletic programs have become primarily commercial—that is, they regularly provide a good or service in exchange for a fee in a market that also includes businesses subject to taxation—rather than educational. To assess the commercial nature of sports programs, the Congressional Budget Office (CBO) first examined the sources of athletic departments' revenue for a subset of colleges and universities and then compared them with the sources of revenue for the schools as a whole. The data indicate that athletic departments at some schools are significantly more commercial than the schools' other activities.

Commercial Activity in Athletic Programs

The analysis focused on athletic departments at schools in Division I of the National Collegiate Athletic Association (NCAA)—a voluntary organization through which colleges and universities govern their sports programs. Division I comprises the schools that have the largest sports programs—they must meet NCAA minimum standards for the number of sports played and for the amount of financial aid awarded to athletes—and are therefore most likely to engage in commercial activities. The division is further divided into three subdivisions—Divisions IA, IAA, and IAAA—that are relevant only for football.[5] To participate in Division IA, schools must meet certain minimum standards for football programs, including home game attendance and scheduled games against other members of the subdivision.

Information on athletic departments' budgets is available for 164 of the 327 schools that were members of Division I in academic year 2004-2005. The data were collected by the *Indianapolis Star* newspaper in 2006. The *Star* requested, under the Freedom of Information Act (FOIA), the budget reports that the NCAA requires from the athletic departments in all schools in Division I. The 112 private schools in the division were exempt from the requests, as were public schools in Pennsylvania and Delaware, by state law.[6]

The *Star* data show that the largest source of athletic departments' revenue is ticket sales, followed by contributions, distributions by athletic conferences of revenue from championship games (including the sale of television rights for those games), and student fees. Large differences exist within the group, however. Division IA schools receive a considerably higher share of revenue from ticket sales (25.4 percent), contributions (20.8 percent), and conference distributions (15.6 percent) than the two other subgroups. That result is not surprising, considering the much higher profile of the football teams in Division IA (see Table 1).

For its analysis of commercialization, CBO divided athletic departments' revenue into two main categories: commercial and noncommercial, described in more detail in Box 1. Revenue received in exchange for goods or services was classified as "commercial" revenue. Commercial sources include income from ticket sales, conference distributions (most of which derive from the sale of the rights to broadcast championship games), sales of team merchandise, and sales from advertisements. Support from the government and the school, the use of the school's facilities, and student fees were classified as "noncommercial."

Contributions to the athletic programs are more difficult to classify than the other sources. Although some contributions are given purely in support of the program, others guarantee the donor a tangible benefit in the form of a good or service. The data specifically count as contributions any amount paid in excess of the face value of a ticket; those excess values are typically paid in return for preferential seating at games. Payments may also be required before a fan can even become eligible to purchase premium tickets to games; such payments are legally considered partially deductible (80 percent) charitable contributions, despite the clear parallel to fee-for-service commercial transactions. The value of some donations of in-kind merchandise, such as apparel and soft drinks, are counted as contributions in the *Star* data, and those gifts represent an exchange in which the donor is paid with advertising and exposure when teams use their products. Contributions to the programs of the schools in Divisions IAA and IAAA, which have a lower profile, are unlikely to be related to premium ticketing or advertising, but over 90 percent of the total contributions to athletic departments go to Division IA schools, at which those factors are likely to be important. Most contributions thus seem to be related to the exchange of goods or services and therefore are primarily commercial. However, because the data do not specify which contributions are associated with a benefit to the donor and which are not, the tables in this report present the commercial share of revenue both with and without contributions.

When contributions are counted as commercial revenue, 73 percent of the revenue of athletic departments for Division I schools comes from commercial sources; when contributions are considered noncommercial, the share is about 54 percent. Within Division I, however, there are dramatic differences. Depending on whether contributions are considered commercial, athletic departments at Division IA schools receive about 60 percent to 80 percent of revenue from commercial sources, compared with 20 percent to 30 percent for schools in Divisions IAA and IAAA.

Table 1. Sources of Revenue for NCAA Division I Athletic Programs, Academic Fiscal Year 2004-2005

Source	Average Revenue (Millions of dollars)				Share of Revenue (Percent)			
	All	IA	IAA	IAAA	All	IA	IAA	IAAA
Commercial[a]								
Ticket sales	5.1	8.9	0.5	0.3	21.9	25.4	5.4	4.1
Conference distributions	3.2	5.5	0.5	0.3	13.7	15.6	4.8	3.8
Advertisements	1.3	2.1	0.3	0.2	5.4	5.8	3.1	3.1
Media rights	0.6	1.1	0	0	2.5	3.0	0.1	0.3
Guarantees	0.6	0.9	0.3	0.1	2.4	2.5	2.8	1.4
Items sold on game day	0.6	1.0	0.1	0	2.4	2.7	0.7	0.6
Investments	0.5	0.8	0.1	0.1	2.0	2.2	1.0	0.6
Sports camp	0.3	0.5	0.2	0.2	1.4	1.3	1.6	1.9
Third-party support	0.1	0.2	0	0	0.5	0.5	0.2	0.3
Other	0.5	0.8	0.2	0.2	2.3	2.4	2.0	2.0
Subtotal	12.7	21.6	2.1	1.4	54.4	61.5	21.7	18.1
Noncommercial								
Student fees	3.1	2.9	3.2	3.6	13.2	8.1	32.6	45.8
Institutional support	2.4	2.5	3.0	1.5	10.4	7.0	31.1	19.2
Facilities and administrative support	0.5	0.6	0.5	0.4	2.2	1.6	5.7	5.2
Government support	0.3	0.4	0.2	0.2	1.2	1.0	1.8	1.9
Subtotal	6.3	6.2	6.9	5.7	27.0	17.7	71.2	72.1
Contributions[b]	4.3	7.3	0.7	0.8	18.6	20.8	7.1	9.8

Table 1. (Continued)

Source	Average Revenue (Millions of dollars)				Share of Revenue (Percent)			
	All	IA	IAA	IAAA	All	IA	IAA	IAAA
Average Total Revenue	**23.3**	**35.2**	**9.7**	**7.9**	**100.0**	**100.0**	**100.0**	**100.0**
Share of Revenue from Commercial Activities								
Contributions counted as noncommercial	n.a.	n.a.	n.a.	n.a.	54.4	61.5	21.7	18.1
Contributions counted as commercial	n.a.	n.a.	n.a.	n.a.	73.0	82.3	28.8	27.9
Memorandum:								
Number of Schools	164	90	41	33				
Total Revenue, All Schools	3,824	3,166	397	261				

Source: Congressional Budget Office based on data included in the budget reports that all Division I schools submit to the National Collegiate Athletic Association for their athletic programs. The data presented here, which include 164 of the 327 schools in Division I in academic fiscal year 2004-2005, were made available in response to a request by the *Indianapolis Star* newspaper under the Freedom of Information Act.

Notes: The academic fiscal year typically runs from July 1 to June 30.

NCAA = National Collegiate Athletic Association; n.a. = not applicable.

a. Defined as revenue received in exchange for goods or services in a market that also includes taxed businesses.

b. Contributions can be commercial or noncommercial.

Commercial Activity in Other University Programs

The share of revenue from commercial activity in the rest of the university serves as a useful benchmark in determining whether athletic departments generate a disproportionately high share of revenue from commercial activity.

The Department of Education maintains the Integrated Postsecondary Education Data System (IPEDS), which contains data on revenue from most postsecondary institutions. CBO used those data to estimate the commercial share of total revenue for the entire school. IPEDS includes a category for revenue earned from auxiliary enterprises, defined as "revenues generated by or collected from the auxiliary enterprise operations of the institution that exist to furnish a service to students, faculty, or staff, and that charge a fee that is directly related to, although not necessarily equal to, the cost of the service."[7] Examples of auxiliary enterprises include residence halls, food services, and athletic departments; all revenue from those sources is classified as commercial.

Many university systems also have hospitals, which serve populations and missions that are somewhat different—though overlapping—from those served by the rest of the university. Although most hospital revenue is received in exchange for services, universities' hospital services are not typically viewed as a commercial enterprise. Whether hospitals should be considered a fundamental part of the universities' educational mission is unclear; the share of revenue from the universities' commercial enterprises shown in Table 2 is therefore presented both with and without hospitals included in the schools' overall revenue. Hospital revenue is classified as noncommercial when included in the universities' total revenue.

With associated university hospitals excluded, the universities as a whole derive almost 11 percent of their revenue from commercial activities when contributions to the university are considered a noncommercial source of revenue. That share rises to about 14 percent when contributions are classified as commercial (see Table 2).[8]

A final consideration is the treatment of athletic programs' revenue within the overall university. For schools in Division IA, that revenue comes primarily from commercial sources, so including it boosts the share of revenue from commercial sources for the university as a whole. Because the IPEDS data do not have a separate category for the revenue of athletic programs, CBO used the *Indianapolis Star* data to estimate each category of revenue net of the effect of athletic programs.[9]

When athletic departments are removed from the calculation of commercial revenue for the university, the commercial share falls (see Table 2). Excluding hospitals, the share of university revenue from commercial sources is about 8 percent when contributions are considered noncommercial. That treatment of contributions may be more appropriate for the rest of the university than for the athletic department, although individuals or organizations making the largest donations to universities also tend to receive something, such as naming rights, in return. When contributions are considered commercial, the share of university revenue from those sources is about 11 percent.[10] Clearly, athletic departments derive a considerably higher share of their revenue from commercial activities than do other parts of universities. Depending on how it is calculated, the share of revenue from commercial sources is seven to eight times higher for Division IA athletic programs than for all other functions at those universities. For Divisions IAA and IAAA, the share of commercial revenue for athletic programs is only two to three times as large as for the universities' other activities (assuming that the extent of commercial activity in those schools, apart from the athletic department, is comparable with that in Division IA schools).

BOX 1. SOURCES OF REVENUE OF ATHLETIC DEPARTMENTS

The data the Congressional Budget Office (CBO) used to determine the sources of revenue of athletic departments in Division I of the National Collegiate Athletic Association (NCAA) are from the request made by the *Indianapolis Star* newspaper under the Freedom of Information Act in 2006. That request was for the budget reports that athletic departments are required to submit to the NCAA. The data include 164 of the 327 schools in Division I in academic year 2004-2005. CBO classified the sources as commercial or noncommercial, as described below; contributions, which can be commercial or noncommercial, were put in a separate category.

Commercial Sources of Revenue

Broadly defined, commercial activities provide a good or service in exchange for a fee in a market that also includes taxed businesses. For this paper, CBO classified the following activities as commercial:

Ticket sales. Ticket sales to the public, faculty, and students and money received for shipping and handling of tickets. Excludes ticket sales for conference and national tournaments.

Conference distributions. Revenue received from participation in bowl games, tournaments, and all NCAA distributions (for example, amounts received for direct participation or through a sharing arrangement with an athletic conference, including shares of conferences' television agreements).

Advertisements. Revenue from corporate sponsorships, sales of advertisements, trademarks, and royalties. Includes the value of in-kind products and services provided as part of a sponsorship (for example, equipment, apparel, soft drinks, water, and isotonic products).

Media rights. Institutional revenue received directly for radio and television broadcasts; Internet and e-commerce rights received through contracts negotiated by the institution.

Guarantees. Revenue received from home teams for participating in away games.

Items sold on game day. Revenue from the sale of programs, novelties, and food or other concessions and from parking fees.

Investments. Distributions from an endowment and other investment income in support of the athletic department.

Sports camp. Amounts received by the athletic department for sports camps and clinics.

Third-party support. All amounts provided by a third party and contractually guaranteed by the institution but not included on the institution's W-2 (for example, a stipend for the use of a car; membership in a country club; allowances for entertainment, clothing, and housing; speaking fees; compensation from camps; and income from radio, television, shoes, and apparel).

Other. Accounts for less than 5 percent of total revenue.

Noncommercial Sources of Revenue

All sources of revenue not meeting the definition of "commercial" were classified as noncommercial:

Student fees. Fees assessed for support of (or the portion of overall fees allocated to) intercollegiate athletics.

Institutional support. Includes the value of institutional resources for the current operations of intercollegiate athletics; all unrestricted funds allocated to the athletic department by the university. That support may include state funds, tuition, tuition waivers, and transfers.

Facilities and administrative support. Includes the value of facilities and services provided by the institution and not charged to the athletic department (for example, an allocation for institutional administrative costs, facilities and maintenance, grounds and field maintenance, security, risk management, utilities, and debt service).

Government support. Includes state, municipal, federal, and other government appropriations made in support of the operations of intercollegiate athletics (including funding specifically earmarked for the athletic department by government agencies for which the institution has no discretion to reallocate).

Contributions

Contributions were defined as amounts received directly from individuals, corporations, associations, foundations, clubs, or other organizations that are designated, restricted, or unrestricted by the donor for the operation of the athletic program. Examples of contributions are amounts paid in excess of a ticket's value (for example, to obtain premium seating), cash, marketable securities, and in-kind contributions. In-kind contributions may include automobiles provided by dealers (measured as the market value of the use of a car), apparel, and soft drinks for use by staff and teams.

Looking at the net income of athletic programs highlights the differences in the commercial nature of programs between the three Division I subgroups (see Table 3). Nearly 99 percent of total net income accrues to Division IA programs, according to the data reported by universities to the NCAA.[11] Average income for programs in Divisions IAA and IAAA is less than a tenth of that in the more commercial Division IA. Those differences in reported income are discussed later in the context of possible policy changes.

Table 2. Sources of Revenue for Schools in NCAA Division IA, Academic Fiscal Year 2004-2005

Source	Including Athletic Department	Excluding Athletic Department
	Total Revenue, by Source (Millions of dollars)	
Commercial		
Auxiliary Enterprises	8,429	6,245
Noncommercial		
Hospitals	9,833	9,833
All other sources	67,389	66,758
Contributions[a]	2,670	1,931
All Sources	**88,321**	**84,768**
	Revenue from Universities' Commercial Activities as a Percentage of Total Revenue	
Excluding Hospitals		
Contributions counted as noncommercial	10.7	8.3
Contributions counted as commercial	14.1	10.9
Including Hospitals		
Contributions counted as noncommercial	9.5	7.4
Contributions counted as commercial	12.6	9.6

Source: Congressional Budget Office based on data from the Department of Education's Integrated Postsecondary Education Data System.

Notes: The academic fiscal year typically runs from July 1 to June 30.

The sample includes the 101 public schools in NCAA Division IA.

NCAA = National Collegiate Athletic Association.

a. Contributions can be commercial or noncommercial.

Table 3. Net Profit or Loss of NCAA Division I Athletic Programs, Academic Fiscal Year 2004-2005

	Number of Programs	Total Net Income or Loss (Millions of dollars)	Subdivision's Share of Total Net Income or Loss (Percent)	Average Income (Millions of dollars)
Division 1A Programs				
With net profit	60	141.4	89.9	2.4
With net loss	24	-34.7	70.4	-1.4
That break even	6	0	0	0
Subtotal	**90**	**106.8**	**98.8**	**1.2**
Division 1AA Programs				
With net profit	22	6.7	4.2	0.3
With net loss	13	-2.6	5.2	-0.2
That break even	6	0	0	0
Subtotal	**41**	**4.1**	**3.8**	**0.1**
Division 1AAA Programs				
With net profit	19	9.2	5.9	0.5
With net loss	12	-12.0	24.4	-1.0
That break even	2	0	0	0
Subtotal	**33**	**-2.8**	**-2.6**	**-0.1**
All Division I Programs				
With net profit	101	157.3	n.a.	1.6
With net loss	49	-49.2	n.a.	-1.0
That break even	14	0	n.a.	0
Total	**164**	**108.1**	**n.a.**	**0.7**

Source: Congressional Budget Office based on data included in the budget reports that all Division I schools submit to the National Collegiate Athletic Association for their athletic departments. The data presented here, which include 164 of the 327 schools in Division I in academic fiscal year 2004-2005, were made available in response to a request by the newspaper the *Indianapolis Star* under the Freedom of Information Act.

Notes: The academic fiscal year typically runs from July 1 to June 30.

There are no rules or even standard practices delineating how schools divide revenue and costs between the athletic department and the university. The profits and losses reported in this table may therefore be a poor guide to the true financial status of athletic departments.

NCAA = National Collegiate Athletic Association; n.a. = not applicable.

Even in that group of elite Division IA programs, however, more than a quarter of the athletic programs report a deficit each year. That result is more likely to reflect the conceptual difficulties in measuring income rather than a statement about the true underlying profitability of those programs. The correct allocation of revenue and expenses to athletic departments, and thus their net profit, is complicated. There are no rules or even standard practices delineating how schools divide revenue from parking, concessions, or licensing, for example, between the athletic department and the university.[12] On the cost side, schools generally list the full standard tuition as the cost of an athletic scholarship, even though that measure overstates the true cost of awarding the scholarship.[13] Because accounting practices vary, the reported profit or loss reported here (in Table 3) may be a poor guide to the true 14 financial status of athletic departments.[14]

Competition with For-Profit Entities

Public and private colleges face relatively little competition from taxable competitors; for-profit postsecondary schools accounted for just 5 percent of total enrollment in degree-granting institutions in 2004.[15] When athletic departments function primarily as a part of the educational experience for students, they participate in that nonprofit market. However, highly competitive college sports teams with large-capacity stadiums and prime-time television events with advertising are more reasonably considered participants in the market for entertainment. They compete for entertainment spending with many other recreational options, but their most direct competitors are professional sports leagues.

Even though competitive university sports programs enter the same market with tax advantages unavailable to the taxable professional leagues, those leagues have never advocated removing tax preferences for the college programs. One reason may be that college sports tend to reduce costs for professional sports.[16] The two sports with the most active and commercial college programs—football and basketball—are each controlled by a single professional association that spends very little on training players. In many cases, all but the final polishing is done by the colleges while the players maintain amateur, non-paid status.[17] If players were not trained by colleges, the professional leagues would probably have to pay those players a salary and complete the training themselves. Particularly in football, the same lack of other leagues in the market—due at least in part to the partial antitrust exemptions granted to the National Football League (NFL)—has also facilitated explicit arrangements between the NCAA and the NFL that avoid direct competition so that they can jointly maximize revenue. For example, college and professional football teams play on different days of the week during the college season. Once the college football season is completed, professional teams play some games on Saturday, the day usually reserved for colleges.

THE BENEFITS OF COLLEGIATE ATHLETICS

Although this analysis focuses on the commercialization of university athletics, the favorable tax treatment of athletic departments within a university might also be evaluated in terms of the social benefit those programs provide to federal taxpayers, who finance the subsidies the universities receive. Research indicates that student athletes tend to underperform academically relative to their credentials, although there is no clear evidence about whether their participation in competitive athletics creates other types of human capital with social benefits.[18] If student athletes reap less academic benefit from higher education than other, similarly qualified students, the admission preferences they currently have represent a misallocation of education resources.

Collegiate athletics, like other extracurricular activities, may also enhance the quality of student life in various nonacademic ways that could also have social benefits. Supporters of university athletic programs cite the leadership skills, teamwork, and dedication that student athletes may learn through their participation.[19] Participating in and watching sporting events can also contribute to an institution's sense of community.

Athletics are unique among extracurricular activities, however, because of the expensive infrastructure support associated with providing such benefits to participants. Although some other activities also require facilities that are expensive to construct and maintain, salaries for coaches are higher than those for almost any other university employee, including college presidents, and no other extracurricular activities are provided with academic tutoring programs like those that focus on maintaining athletic eligibility.[20]

Athletic programs might also provide ancillary benefits (in addition to any direct profit from the programs themselves) to the schools, allowing them to further their mission of higher education. Athletic programs could benefit schools indirectly by improving their name recognition or reputation.[21] Successful athletic programs could also encourage increased giving by alumni to a school or improve the quality of the entering class by increasing the number of students who apply for admission. Although various empirical studies on both of those points have come to conflicting conclusions, overall the evidence indicates that the effect of successful programs on either of those measures at a specific school is likely to be positive but small (see the appendix).

Applying those conclusions to all university athletic programs in the nation—the appropriate level at which to evaluate a federal subsidy—is difficult. Most studies look at the relationship between success, defined by win-loss records or championship wins, and alumni giving or the number of applications at a specific school. Because athletic success is in general a zero-sum endeavor (championship games always have a winner), the relationships that hold for a single or small group of athletic programs may not hold for all athletic programs in the nation. There is no evidence suggesting that athletic programs increase the overall amount of charitable contributions (as opposed to shifting them between different schools or other nonprofit organizations) or the average quality of students attending all colleges.[22] Furthermore, the effect of athletic programs on either of those measures seems likely to be dwarfed by that of the many other federal subsidies for charitable giving and higher education. In fact, the current subsidy to athletic departments may simply encourage an "arms race" between schools, in which universities spend increasing resources on measures of athletic success that, at most, benefit their own institutions at the expense of others. Encouraging such competition within the higher education sector seems unlikely to benefit the federal taxpayers that ultimately pay for the subsidy.

POLICY OPTIONS

If the Congress decided that some or all of the activities undertaken by college athletic programs are primarily commercial, the rationale for providing preferential tax treatment to those activities would be eliminated or greatly reduced. Changes to the tax preferences could be achieved in one or more of the following ways:

- Limiting the deduction of charitable contributions,

- Limiting the use of tax-exempt bonds, or
- Limiting the exemption from income taxation, either for all or for certain types of income.

Several issues might arise if the Congress decided to eliminate or reduce those tax preferences. Most important, the position of athletic departments within larger nonprofit institutions affords many opportunities for shifting contributions, other revenue, or expenditures from one part of the university to another. The budgetary relationship between universities and their constituent parts would significantly reduce the effectiveness of most attempts to limit the general tax preferences for athletics while leaving those for the entire university intact. More targeted changes, such as limiting the types of income statutorily exempt from the unrelated business income tax, are more likely to have an impact but would still require assessing the commercialization of all of the university's activities rather than just those of the athletic department.

Limiting the Deduction of Charitable Contributions

Under the Internal Revenue Code, donors to college sports programs may deduct their contributions from their federal adjusted gross income. Many of those contributions, however, are made in order to become eligible to purchase game tickets or to ensure access to premium seating. In effect, the transaction is an exchange of money for valuable rights, and the benefits of the contribution accrue to the donor. Under current law, the donor may nonetheless deduct 80 percent of the value of such contributions.

If the Congress decided that contributions to athletic departments are primarily commercial, it could specify that contributions to universities' sports programs or to foundations that support them—either contributions given in exchange for certain benefits or all contributions—may not be deducted on the donor's federal tax return. Money can easily be moved between departments within the university, however, and a university administration can allocate a greater share of its own budget to its sports program. If that fact is well understood by donors and administrators, donations to sports programs might be unaffected by such a policy change; lower explicit donations to the athletic programs could simply be offset by indirect donations through the university.

Although such a response might completely offset the effects of a change in the deductibility of contributions, it would probably not do so. Total donations would be likely to decline to some extent, and a school's response would determine how the effects of that decline were shared between the athletic program and other parts of the budget.

Limiting the Use of Tax-Exempt Bonds

Although contributions can be given to or earmarked for sports programs directly, athletic departments generally do not have borrowing authority that is separate from that of the college or university as a whole. The borrowing is undertaken on behalf of the school and is earmarked for the sports program in the tax-exempt bond offering.

It would thus be more difficult for schools to move borrowing that is earmarked for another part of the university to the athletic department if the Congress prohibited the use of tax-exempt bonds to finance the capital facilities of sports programs. Even so, it might be possible for the university to borrow indirectly for the sports program. If the university could not use the proceeds from bonds directly for the sports program, it could still borrow for capital spending in other areas that would have been financed with operating revenue and use that operating revenue to finance the sports facilities. The major problem would be the large amount of revenue needed—the university might not have adequate capital facilities being financed with operating revenue to make the substitution. Thus, eliminating the direct use of tax-exempt bonds for sports facilities would be unlikely to eliminate their use but would probably have a bigger effect on the total amount of bonds a university issues than the elimination of charitable contributions would have on total charitable contributions.

Limiting the Exemption from Income Taxation

Attempts to end the exemption from income taxation for athletic departments would probably encourage universities to undertake significant efforts to avoid taxes. A sports program's position within a much larger institution makes successful taxation of its true net income a difficult undertaking. Changing the treatment of income from specific sources, such as royalty income or income from corporate sponsorships, might be effective, especially if the changes applied to the entire university rather than just the athletic program.

Subject the Income of Athletic Programs to the UBIT. The Congress could, by statute, reclassify collegiate athletic programs as unrelated commercial entities operated by a nonprofit organization, thereby subjecting them to the unrelated business income tax.[23] Because an athletic program in a nonprofit private or public postsecondary institution is part of a much larger economic entity that would remain classified as a nonprofit, the institution would have a substantial incentive to shift costs from the untaxed portion of the university to the taxable portion and to shift income in the other direction. Increased net income would have no tax consequences for the untaxed sector, and increased costs would reduce or eliminate taxable net income for the athletic program.[24]

Universities have other means of eliminating taxable income if cost shifting failed to do so completely. Unlike a for-profit enterprise, which has shareholders who expect managers to distribute a surplus as dividends or retain the surplus and distribute it in the future as capital gains, the nonprofit or public enterprise has no shareholders. If athletic programs still showed a profit even after income or cost shifting, that profit could be reduced or eliminated in two ways. First, the program could increase costs by paying higher wages to coaches or administrators or by spending more for other items, such as athletic facilities.[25] Second, the program could reduce revenues—for example, by lowering the price of game tickets. Directors of athletic programs might prefer to use one of those alternatives rather than pay taxes; all of the alternatives would reduce the income subject to tax.

Restructure the Relationship Between Athletic Departments and the University. The schools' ability to shift income from one part of their budget to another is likely to prevent the net income of collegiate athletic programs from being taxed. To prevent such shifting, the Congress could require that the financial relationship between athletic programs judged to be commercial and their universities be severed completely. Like any commercial entity, the athletic programs could still lower their tax liability by reducing revenue or increasing costs, but they would be limited in doing so by their need to raise capital.

Such a major restructuring of the relationship between athletic departments and universities would present a variety of practical and political issues. Perhaps most important, it would be extremely difficult to implement effectively at the public universities that host most of the major sports teams. The Congress has made many changes to the exemption for nonprofit institutions, including imposing the unrelated business income tax. But the IRS has considered every commercial activity undertaken by a state or local government to be an essential public service and therefore not subject to taxation. Taxing a public entity would raise legal issues with regard to intergovernmental tax immunity. At the moment, the tax law treats nonprofit and public enterprises very differently. Therefore, a state institution of higher education operating a sports program classified as a commercial enterprise would be subject to the UBIT under that approach, but a state operating the identical sports program as a state entity not affiliated with its public university would not.

Reclassify Certain Types of Income. Instead of attempting to classify all net income from athletic programs as commercial and subject to the UBIT, the Congress could consider reclassifying certain types of income typically earned by those programs as unrelated income. For example, an athletic program earns royalty income when it receives a payment in exchange for allowing a for-profit enterprise to use its name. Current law excludes all royalty income from the UBIT because such income is considered passive. In general, passive income, which also includes income from investments, is not considered commercial because it is not derived from direct competition with commercial enterprises.

Some types of royalty income may reasonably be considered more commercial than others. The royalty income derived from the ownership of mineral and oil rights is usually a clear example of passive income; universities own the land to which such rights are attached but have little or no involvement in the ongoing commercial activity that occurs. In contrast, when colleges and universities license team names, mottoes, and other trademarks to for-profit businesses that supply apparel, accessories, and credit cards to the general public, they approve each product and use of their symbols and, in some cases, exchange information, such as donor lists, with the licensees to aid in their marketing. In 2005, the collegiate sector earned $203 million in that type of licensing revenue.[26] The manufacture or sale of such items would clearly be commercial—and subject to the UBIT—if undertaken directly by the schools. Schools' active involvement in generating licensing income could be the basis for considering such income as commercial and therefore subject to the UBIT. Even the income from mineral rights has been determined taxable if the university is substantially involved in the daily operation of such properties.

Bringing royalty income that accrues only to athletic departments under the UBIT would be problematic, however, for several reasons. First, schools could simply limit their licensing of the names and trademarks of their athletic teams and increase their licensing of the school's name and trademarks to minimize the amount of taxable activity, although doing so would be likely to decrease sales. More important, if royalty income from licensing team names to for-profit businesses was truly considered commercial and subject to the UBIT, the same arguments would apply in full force to licensing all other university names and trademarks. A consistent policy would subject all such income to the UBIT because of its commercial nature. Such a change in policy could affect many other nonprofits in addition to colleges and universities, although the amount of all commercial activity in athletic departments relative to that undertaken by universities and other nonprofits does provide a rationale for different treatment.

Income from corporate sponsorship is also explicitly excluded from the UBIT. Generally, sponsorship income arises from corporate payments made in exchange for associating the corporate name with the nonprofit or public institution. In the context of college athletics, most major college championship games, stadiums, and arenas have a corporate sponsor whose name is included in the name of the event or facility. The IRS considered subjecting such income to the UBIT in 1991. In the Taxpayer Relief Act of 1997, however, the Congress responded by excluding "qualified sponsorship payments" from the UBIT, defining such payments as those in return for no other benefit than the acknowledgment of the sponsor. The law makes a distinction between payments in return for advertising (which includes descriptions of the sponsor's products, locations, or other features) and payments in return for adding the sponsor's name to an event or facility (which is not considered a substantial benefit). The NCAA estimated that corporate sponsorship payments to all athletic programs totaled $275 million in academic year 2004-2005.[27]

The fact that sponsors of athletic facilities and bowl games are willing to pay large sums in qualified sponsorship payments suggests that they derive some benefit from the prominent location and display of their corporate trademarks during athletic contests and national broadcasts. If the Congress decided that those benefits were essentially similar to those conferred by advertising as defined in the law, it could reclassify such payments as taxable income from an unrelated business. Such a determination would be supported not only by the commercial nature of those specific transactions but also by the commercial nature of athletic departments themselves, in contrast to other nonprofits that earn some revenue from similar sources while remaining financed primarily by noncommercial activities.

However, not all payments for naming rights at athletic facilities really are in return for a substantial benefit; the benefit to the sponsor varies considerably among schools and is of course largest for the few schools whose athletic arenas attract extremely large crowds and host widely televised events. The range of success among programs—and thus the benefit in being a sponsor—implies that a blanket determination of "substantial benefit" from all sponsorships could be unreasonable. The situation is clearer in the case of sponsors of championship games. Title sponsors of widely televised events such as bowl games clearly receive a substantial benefit from their sponsorship. If the Congress determined that such transactions are commercial, it could specifically classify sponsorship payments for those particular athletic contests as taxable income.

Even reclassifying certain types of income might fail to be effective if the policy was intended to apply only to athletic departments. Unless the treatment of such income was consistent across the entire university, strong incentives would remain to shift income taxable to the athletic department to the nontaxed portion of the university. However, reclassifying certain types of income as unrelated, and therefore taxable, would have the advantage of focusing directly on the types of revenue that are associated with the relatively few highly commercial athletic departments rather than on the majority of athletic departments that engage in little commercial activity.

Appendix: Research on Certain Benefits of Intercollegiate Sports

Although the extent of commercialization in college sports provides one basis for evaluating athletic programs' access to federal subsidies intended for nonprofit organizations, other factors may also play a role. For example, many supporters of university athletics argue that a successful athletic department creates benefits for colleges and universities that are then passed on to the students. Numerous studies have attempted to prove or disprove that notion.

Athletic success is generally thought to benefit schools in one of two ways: by increasing donations to the school or by increasing the pool of applicants for admission. Research on the relationship between athletics and donations has used a variety of measures of athletic success and has come to conflicting conclusions. One study, for example, found that winning percentages in the major sports did not have a significant effect on donations.[28]

A larger study reached a similar conclusion regarding winning records, but the authors documented a positive relationship between giving and appearances in championship games.[29] Using a panel data set of 320 institutions, a third study concluded that postseason success in football and basketball leads to increased gifts restricted for the use of the athletic department for some schools but no increase in unrestricted giving to the university.[30] Another study, using detailed data from a single large university, found little relationship between teams' general success and donations but found a significant increase in donations for some alumni when a sport in which they had participated was successful.[31] Overall, those studies seem to indicate that postseason success may increase restricted donations to the athletic department by particular alumni but that the effect on total giving to the university is likely to be small.

The results of research on the relationship between athletic success and the quality of entering classes are equally inconsistent. One study documented a positive relationship between advancing in the National Collegiate Athletic Association (NCAA) basketball tournament and Scholastic Aptitude Test (SAT) scores for the entering class.[32] In contrast, another study found that championships increased the number of applications but had no effect on the SAT scores or grades of entering students.[33] A comprehensive study of the effects of athletic success on the quality of incoming students concluded that the percentage of games won was positively correlated with the quality of the students but that the effect was generally small and statistically insignificant; the authors also reached similar conclusions about the relationship between winning and alumni donations.[34] Another paper examined a separate mechanism through which athletic success could provide benefits to public schools—increased state funding. The author found that schools with a Division IA football program receive significantly more in state funding than those without one but that an increase in the success of the program does not raise the amount of appropriations it receives.[35]

Although the studies reach conflicting conclusions, even in the studies that find that successful athletic programs have a positive impact on the school overall, the measured impacts are generally quite small. In addition, studies that demonstrate a positive impact for a single school or a subset of schools do not address whether success in intercollegiate athletics increases donations or student quality at all schools—or simply shifts them between schools.

End Notes

[1] Claudia Goldin and Lawrence F. Katz (*Long Run Changes in the U.S. Wage Structure: Narrowing, Widening, Polarizing*, Working Paper No. 13568 [Cambridge, Mass.: National Bureau of Economic Research, November 2007]) document a rise in the return to education in general over the past several decades and, in particular, a rise in the return to postsecondary education. David M. Cutler and Adriana Lleras-Muney ("Education and Health: Evaluating Theories and Evidence," in Robert F. Schoeni and others, eds., *Making Americans Healthier: Social and Economic Policy as Health Policy* [New York: Russell Sage Foundation, 2008]) discuss the evidence for a positive relationship between education and health outcomes, with particular attention to the mechanisms through which education may be the cause of better health.

[2] Eric Hanushek and Ludgar Woessmann (*Do Better Schools Lead to More Growth? Cognitive Skills, Economic Outcomes, and Causation*, Working Paper No. 14633 [Cambridge, Mass.: National Bureau of Economic Research, January 2009]) find empirical evidence of a causal relationship between educational attainment and economic growth rates across countries. For a discussion of the relationship between postsecondary education and social mobility, see Robert Haveman and Timothy Smeeding, "The Role of Higher Education in Social Mobility," *Future of Children*, vol. 16, no. 2 (2006), pp. 125–150.

[3] Because the corporate income tax limits the deduction that corporate donors can take for their charitable donations, a commercial entity whose income accrues directly to a nonprofit parent would, in the absence of the UBIT, pay lower taxes than a business that simply donated all of its profits to a nonprofit organization.

[4] A previous Congressional Budget Office report, *Taxing the Untaxed Business Sector*, Background Paper (July 2005), discussed how those institutions are similar to for-profit businesses in important ways.

[5] The NCAA has recently replaced the names IA, IAA, and IAAA with Football Bowl Subdivision, Football Championship Subdivision, and Division I Non-football, respectively. This paper uses the older terminology for brevity.

[6] Very little information is available regarding the budgets of athletic departments at nonprofit private schools. Those schools and their athletic departments receive the same preferential tax treatment as public schools. The current lack of publicly available information about their programs makes a similar evaluation of their commercialization impossible and could be one justification for mandating additional disclosure of budget information from institutions registered as nonprofits.

[7] Susan G. Broyles, *IPEDS Glossary* (Department of Education, National Center for Education Statistics, rev. August 1995), http://nces.ed.gov/pubs95/95822.pdf, p. 28.

[8] When hospitals are included in the calculation, the commercial share of revenue is 9.5 percent with contributions considered noncommercial and 12.6 percent with contributions considered commercial.

[9] In adjusting the universities' revenue to exclude revenue from athletic departments, CBO assumed that the schools that did not respond to the FOIA request were similar to those that did. CBO made the adjustment using averages from the *Indianapolis Star* data. For example, the calculation for all university revenue excluding athletics was made by subtracting the average revenue of athletic departments in the *Star* data, multiplied by the number of schools (101), from the total university revenue given in IPEDS. CBO used a similar process to calculate university revenue excluding athletics for contributions and auxiliary enterprises, using the *Star* data averages for contributions to athletic departments and commercial revenue from athletic departments, respectively.

[10] Including hospitals, universities derive about 7 percent of revenue from commercial sources when contributions are considered noncommercial and 10 percent of revenue from commercial sources when contributions are considered commercial.

[11] The majority of income is, of course, reinvested directly into the athletic programs—for example, into compensation for coaches and administrators. Because the athletes retain amateur status, there are strict limits on their compensation, and they are barred from receiving benefits that are proportional to the income that they earn for the university. Robert W. Brown and R. Todd Jewell ("Measuring Marginal Revenue Product in College Athletics: Updated Estimates," in John Fizel and Rodney Fort, eds., *Economics of College Sports* [Westport, Conn.: Praeger, 2004], pp. 153–162) estimate that universities earn $400,000 from each high-performing football player and over $1 million from each high-performing basketball player.

[12] Robert Sandy and Peter Sloane, "Why Do U.S. Colleges Have Sports Programs?" in Fizel and Fort, eds., *Economics of College Sports*, pp. 87–110.

[13] If class sizes are fixed, the cost of granting a scholarship to an athlete is the tuition that would have been paid by another student who cannot now be admitted, and the majority of students do not pay the listed tuition because they receive financial aid in the form of tuition discounting or grants. See Burton A. Weisbrod, Jeffrey P. Ballou, and Evelyn D. Asch, *Mission and Money: Understanding the University* (Cambridge, U.K.: Cambridge University Press, 2008), Chapter 5. If class sizes are not fixed, the cost of granting a scholarship to an athlete could be even less than the net tuition that would be paid by another student, because the athlete's admission does not prevent any other applicant from being admitted.

[14] The profitability of collegiate sports is a matter of continuing debate. On the one hand, Andrew Zimbalist (*Unpaid Professionals: Commercialism and Conflict in Big-Time College Sports* [Princeton, N.J.: Princeton University Press, 1999], Chapter 7) estimates that although the top dozen programs run persistent surpluses and some others may turn a profit during a particularly successful year, the average program runs a deficit of $710,000 per year once adjustments for some of the reporting problems discussed in the text are made. On the other hand, Brian Goff ("Effects of University Athletics on the University: A Review and Extension of Empirical Assessment," *Journal of Sport Management*, vol. 14, no. 2 [2000]) estimates that only 10 percent of the top 109 programs lose money in a year. He concludes that public universities may underestimate profits by $800,000 per program and that private schools underestimate profits by even more.

[15] U.S. Department of Education, *Digest of Education Statistics*, http://nces.ed.gov/programs/digest/d07/tables/dt07_185.asp.

[16] College baseball is an exception in that it competes for players with the minor leagues; even so, the collegiate and professional baseball seasons do not overlap the majority of the time.

[17] The lack of compensation for college athletes (despite the substantial revenue that they earn for the university) is one factor encouraging basketball players to forgo college and instead improve their skills in professional leagues in other countries before returning to play for a professional team in the United States. If more athletes decided to play for foreign professional leagues rather than for colleges, the result could be both a decline in the commercialization of college basketball and a decline in its value to the domestic professional league.

[18] See, for example, William G. Bowen and Sarah A. Levin, *Reclaiming the Game: College Sports and Educational Values* (Princeton, N.J.: Princeton University Press, 2003), Chapter 6. The authors concluded that after accounting for the influence of race, field of study, individual scores on the Scholastic Aptitude Test (SAT), and the average SAT score at the institution, athletes who are recruited achieve lower class rank relative to their academic credentials than do walk-on athletes or the general student body. The effect is most pronounced among football players and rowers. Others have noted that graduation rates for football and basketball team members in Division I are considerably lower than those for nonathletes or for athletes in other sports. See Weisbrod, Ballou, and Asch, *Mission and Money*, p. 231.

[19] Letter from Myles Brand, President of the National Collegiate Athletic Association, to the Honorable William Thomas (November 13, 2006), *www.ncaa.org/wps/ncaa*? ContentID=44636, p. 4.

[20] For a comparison of coaches' and university presidents' salaries, see Weisbrod, Ballou, and Asch, *Mission and Money*, pp. 221 and 251–277. For a discussion of spending on tutoring programs for athletes, which the NCAA requires of all Division I schools, see Zimbalist, *Unpaid Professionals*, pp. 43–44.

[21] Goff, "Effects of University Athletics on the University," p. 91.

[22] Total charitable donations to all sectors have remained roughly 2 percent of disposable income over time, suggesting that increased donations to higher education are offset by decreased giving to other nonprofits (Weisbrod, Ballou, and Asch, *Mission and Money*, p. 36).

[23] For an in-depth discussion of the legal argument for applying the UBIT to college athletics under current law, see John D. Colombo, "The NCAA, Tax Exemption, and College Athletics" (*University of Illinois Law Review*, forthcoming; also available at http://papers.ssrn.com/abstract=1336727).

[24] Joseph J. Cordes and Burton A. Weisbrod ("Differential Taxation of Nonprofits and the Commercialization of Nonprofit Revenues," in Burton A. Weisbrod, ed., *To Profit or Not To Profit* [Cambridge, U.K.: Cambridge University Press, 1998]) conclude that nonprofits subject to the UBIT may shift expenses that are up to one-third of their gross profit to the taxable portion of the entity.

[25] The large number of programs that currently post a loss (see Table3) may suggest that those behaviors already occur; administrators and coaches may be able to extract higher salaries from those nonprofit programs because such programs have no incentive to show a profit.

[26] Weisbrod, Ballou, and Asch, *Mission and Money*, p. 245.

[27] Letter from Myles Brand to the Honorable William Thomas (November 13, 2006).

[28] Paul W. Grimes and George A. Chressanthis, "Alumni Contributions to Academics: The Role of Intercollegiate Sports and NCAA Sanctions," *American Journal of Economics and Sociology*, vol. 53, no. 1 (1994), pp. 27–40.

[29] Robert Baade and Jeffery Sundberg, "Fourth Down and Gold to Go? Assessing the Link Between Athletics and Alumni Giving," *Social Science Quarterly*, vol. 77, no. 4 (1996), pp. 789–803.

[30] Brad R. Humphreys and Michael Mondello, "Intercollegiate Athletic Success and Donations at NCAA Division I Institutions," *Journal of Sport Management*, vol. 21, no. 2 (April 2007).

[31] Jonathan Meer and Harvey S. Rosen, *The Impact of Athletic Performance on Alumni Giving: An Analysis of Micro Data*, Working Paper No. 13937 (Cambridge, Mass.: National Bureau of Economic Research, April 2008).

[32] Franklin G. Mixon Jr., "Athletics versus Academics? Rejoining the Evidence from SAT Scores," *Education Economics*, vol. 3, no. 3 (December 1995), pp. 277–283.

[33] J. Douglas Toma and Michael Cross, "Intercollegiate Athletics and Student College Choice: Understanding the Impact of Championship Seasons on the Quantity and Quality of Undergraduate Applicants" (paper presented at the 21st Annual Meeting of the Association for the Study of Higher Education, Memphis, Tenn., October 30–November 2, 1996).

[34] Robert E. Litan, Jonathan M. Orszag, and Peter R. Orszag, *The Empirical Effects of Collegiate Athletics: An Interim Report* (prepared by Sebago Associates for the National Collegiate Athletic Association, August 2003), www.ncaa.org/databases/baselineStudy/ baseline.pdf.

[35] Brad R. Humphreys, "The Relationship Between Big-Time College Football and State Appropriations for Higher Education," *International Journal of Sport Finance*, vol. 1, no. 2 (May 2006).

CHAPTER SOURCES

The following chapters have been previously published:

Chapter 1 – This is an edited reformatted and augmented version of a Congressional Research Service publication, report R41060, dated February 1, 2010.

Chapter 2 – This is an edited reformatted and augmented version of a Congressional Research Service publication, report R41294, dated June 22, 2010.

Chapter 3 – This is an edited reformatted and augmented version of a Congressional Budget Office publication, dated May 2009.

Index

A

B

C

I

J

L

M

N

O

U

V

W